RESET

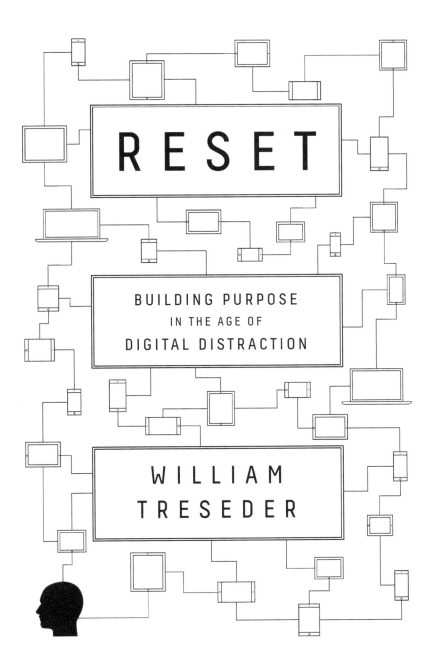

RESET

BUILDING PURPOSE
IN THE AGE OF
DIGITAL DISTRACTION

WILLIAM TRESEDER

LIONCREST
PUBLISHING

RESET

Building Purpose in the Age of Digital Distraction

ISBN   978-1-5445-1160-3 *Paperback*

978-1-5445-1159-7 *Ebook*

For my mother, who helped me and so many others find our voices.

CONTENTS

INTRODUCTION

WHY DO I NEED TO RESET?

"Work is hard. Distractions are plentiful. And time is short."
—ADAM HOCHSCHILD, AMERICAN AUTHOR

We are living in a scary new world. A digital world.

Everything is changing: the jobs we have; the friends we choose; the hobbies we pursue; and the time we invest. We are living through a societal earthquake.

Each of us is living through this massive shift in intensely emotional, often disruptive, ways. We feel stuck, left behind, angry, afraid, and frustrated. Why? Because this isn't what we were taught to expect out of life. Because we are being tested in new and surprising ways. And because so far, most of us aren't taking advantage of the opportunities that we keep hearing about.

The common thread that connects us is that we were not prepared in any way for the digital world, or its endless stream of distractions. And how could we be prepared? Our parents had no idea what was coming. Neither did our teachers, friends, or coworkers.

So we simply don't have the right tools to thrive in this new environment. Not yet, anyway.

THE PROBLEM

The digital world makes it easier than ever to consume information, while also expanding the range of options at our fingertips (literally). We get trapped in all this information, like a mosquito in amber. For most of us, our default setting is becoming mindless, passive consumption.

Everyone in this digital world is swimming in a vast ocean of information, conveniently packaged to hook us. And we are swallowing it! Then we get dragged down by a digital flood of texts, comments, videos, notifications, movies, posts, shows, articles, threads, and on and on and on.

Don't believe me? Ask yourself one question and stop

reading if it doesn't resonate with you. Here it is: when was the last time you looked up from a screen and couldn't believe how much time had passed?

I rest my case.

And you aren't alone, believe me. All of us are suffering the same fate. We all feel the itch to pull out our phone every time there is the slightest pause in our day. Assuming, of course, we aren't staring at it already.

No one asked to become citizens of the digital world. There are no classes, no training, no certificates. No naturalization ceremony. At some point, someone hands us a laptop or a phone, then we just...start using it. And we quickly become addicted to these devices and the bite-sized brain treats they dispense to us.

If we aren't careful, we will spend the rest of our lives this way.

ALONE AND AFRAID

The saddest part of our current situation is that each of us is suffering in isolation. We are struggling to figure out what works by ourselves. Why? Because the digital world is so new that we don't have a set of rules for adapting to and thriving in this environment.

Traditional institutions will not help us. Our systems of education and business were built for an older era. The mindsets and behaviors that we learned were all about the golden age of big industries, where conformity and efficiency dominated. Back then, we were expected to keep our heads down, grinding away at work until we retired into sun- and golf-soaked irrelevance.

But that fantasy is no longer an option for us. Things change, and so must we. Eventually, each of us will face the harsh truth: we are struggling in the digital world.

Most of us already sense this and are trying to figure out the solution on our own. Ironically, this journey involves diving deeper into the world of infinite information. We read articles, listen to podcasts, talk with our friends, and then settle on a few changes we hope will make the difference. We may avoid answering emails for a few weekends or try to unplug during our next vacation.

This is the equivalent of a New Year's resolution. Things might look good for a few days or even weeks. Eventually, however, your plan will disintegrate despite the best intentions. Why? Because a few uncoordinated tactical changes won't save you from the world-class advertising machinery that wants to steal every second of your attention.

Unfortunately, the reality is that you probably won't

stumble onto a sustainable strategy that addresses the root problem. For that, you must uncover and confront fundamental issues.

This personal transformation is the purpose of this book. That's what it means to Reset: to help lead you to the point where you begin building your purpose. To systematically change your mindset from one of scarcity to one of abundance. To shift your habits and daily routines toward consistent action.

It won't be easy, but the goal is a worthy one: conquering distraction and living a life of purpose.

Success in the digital world can reward you like nothing else. You can develop skills that you never dreamed of, the confidence to tackle new challenges with enthusiasm, and the experience required to live a complete life. You can wake up feeling on fire to pursue each day's unique opportunities. You can impact the lives of millions of people. You can leave behind a legacy that will inspire others. You can exploit the digital world, instead of being exploited by it!

We all *sort of* understand the situation. We *sort of* see how much our daily lives are changing. We *sort of* believe that the world is fundamentally different than it was a few generations ago.

Sort of is not enough. We must believe. We must commit. Only then can we live the principles of this book. Then we can experience the digital world in a different way. We can feel the changes in our bodies, minds, and souls when we have a clear and compelling mission, a bias toward taking action, and a daily structure that reinforces our goals.

If any of this rings true for you, then read this book. Everything will change when you start putting these ideas into practice.

A LITTLE ABOUT ME

How do I know? Because everything changed for me. I started taking advantage of the digital world years ago, mostly by an accident of my military service. I saw the effects of technology while serving in Iraq and Afghanistan as a United States Marine. People's lives were literally transformed before my eyes through access to information. They went from sitting in remote, mud-walled homes to checking email in the blink of an eye!

The quest to understand technology's impact on us led me to Singularity University, where I worked with some of the world's most accomplished entrepreneurs and futurists. There, I learned about the accelerating momentum and power of technology. This paired with my research at Stanford, studying how our lives change with each new wave of technology products. It wasn't just academic, either. During college, I deployed to Iraq and Afghanistan, which forced me to test my thinking against the harsh realities of war.

After graduating, I dove headfirst into building a series of successful businesses. Right now, my work is split between running entrepreneurial ecosystems around the world at NeuBridges and helping the military solve its most difficult problems by working with Silicon Valley's best and brightest engineers through BMNT.

The military and startups are wildly different environments. The cultures, dress, language, and worldviews diverge in many ways. I wasn't expecting to find a common thread running through them. But I was very wrong.

I learned something simple and profound from my years of experience at the seam of technology entrepreneurship and national security. Two of the most demanding activities on the planet share some common ground. Both cultures learned to foster the same things, albeit for very different reasons.

What is this powerful truth? Simply this: your mindset and daily habits are the most important predictors of your ability to live in a fulfilling way. No matter the environment—from war to business—we can create purpose every day through our actions.

It is this purpose that will sustain us in the face of the digital world's distractions. A deep, fulfilling purpose is the only lasting cure.

These words are easy to write, and yet incredibly hard to put into practice. But once we get the foundation right, everything else falls in line.

I wrote this book to walk people through this difficult process and help them take practical steps to improve their daily lives in the face of endless distractions. Instead of guessing, I want you to take the best of what already works from other brilliant and inspirational people, cutting-edge research, and personal experience. Use the parts that resonate with you. Toss out the rest.

Reset flows through four phases, each one building on the last. In Part I: Challenge—Chapters One through Four—we will explore the nature of the digital world, especially its educational, social, and financial dimensions. We will finish Part I with a better picture of why and how the world is changing so quickly.

In Part II: Inspiration—Chapters Five and Six—we will dive into the inspiration and logic for your Reset. We will learn from people and organizations who have already walked this path. This part points us in the right direction.

In Part III: Foundation—Chapters Seven, Eight, and Nine—we will discuss the principles that let us adapt successfully to the digital world. We will see the hidden value of mission, action, and structure. These three powerful concepts are the open secrets of a few visionaries who already figured out the digital world!

In Part IV: Method—Chapters Ten through Sixteen—we will walk through your unique path toward fulfillment. We will construct a plan to increase your sense of purpose while minimizing the distractions that threaten to overwhelm us every day.

The chapters in this book follow a pattern. Each one starts with a question, a prompt that orients us on the material. Then we explore the question with stories and analysis that make up the bulk of the material. Finally, we close with a recap of the key concepts, some follow-up practices, and additional resources if you are interested in learning more. Then, in Part IV, you will also find specific guidance that will channel your enthusiasm into useful changes in your mindset and behavior.

This book will help you get perspective on your own life and the challenges you face. You will find common ground with the people in these stories. You will also learn both the *Why?* and *How?* to begin adapting your behavior to the digital world. Especially the daily re-creation of your purpose.

By the end of the book, we will see how the right combination of mission, action, and structure helps both you and the people you care about. That's right: even your family and friends will benefit from your Reset. This mutually guaranteed success is part of the beauty of the digital world. Everyone can win!

I want you to *do* this book, not read it. I want you to grab this opportunity to start transforming your mindset and habits.

We're going to see how we adapt to—and thrive in—this new digital world. We will learn the surprising truths about evolving from a life of distraction to one of purpose. From consumption to creation. From passive to active. From the trivial to the significant.

This transition to purposeful action, especially in the service of others, is the secret to success in the twenty-first century. I hope you're ready to earn your place!

Throughout the book, you will see citation numbers to note a resource was used. You can find the links to the sources at theresetbook.com/tools.

PART I

THE CHALLENGE

CHAPTER ONE

CHOKE

WHERE DOES ALL MY TIME GO?

"It's named the 'Web' for good reason."

—DAVID FOSTER WALLACE, AMERICAN AUTHOR

A swipe on your phone. Or a quick tap on your watch. That's all it takes to start choking.

I was having a great morning at work recently. Everything was breaking my way. I had a good night's sleep. My kids behaved themselves as they got dressed and had breakfast. My wife and I had a soft kiss before we parted ways. I felt energetic and optimistic. I was flying through all the stuff I needed to get done.

A great morning by almost anyone's standards.

Then it all went sideways. I was finishing a sentence and needed to use the word "unnecessary," but couldn't remember the spelling. Was it one c and two s's, or the other way around?

Yes, I could just type it and wait for the red squiggly line to tell me if I was wrong. I know that, but I am weird about stuff like this. I wanted to guess the spelling, then verify the spelling by using an online dictionary. Then I could see if there was something cool I could learn about the word that would help me remember the correct spelling next time.

Like I said, I'm weird.

So I did what anyone would do. I opened a new browser tab, googled "unnecessary," and started reading. Of course, it didn't stop there. Before I knew it, I was watching some YouTube video about the first successful launch and landing of a SpaceX rocket.[1] And then another video. And then another.

When I finally shook myself out of this trance, I had wasted forty-five minutes! What started with the spelling and etymology of "unnecessary" had morphed into SpaceX rockets, and then ended with me watching a *Drunk History* episode with Will Ferrell as Abraham Lincoln and Don Cheadle as Frederick Douglass.[2]

Don't get me wrong, the *Drunk History* video was hilarious. I was laughing loudly. But that video had absolutely nothing to do with what I wanted to accomplish. My goals for the day were still laid out in front of me, untouched. The day's momentum was completely erased. So of course, I started beating up on myself for getting distracted.

Sound familiar? How often do you end up being knocked off track by a stream of irrelevant—but "free"—content? That, my friends, is choking: mindlessly consuming information that is unrelated to your goal at that moment.

We all know the most common choking position. Both hands are hovering over the keys, with thumbs perched like little gargoyles. Your head is tilted down at a forty-five-degree angle, staring intently. You are completely oblivious to the rest of the world.

This is the official posture of the twenty-first century.

DISTRACTIONS EVERYWHERE

We are tempted to choke just about everywhere, all the time. The digital world always has one more interesting thing for us to look at. Texts, emails, posts, pins, tweets, likes, favorites, features, alerts, flashes, quick reads, promoted ads, suggested friends, comments, trending topics, numbered lists, banner ads, skims, news briefs, takeaways, FYIs—on and on it goes.

Life is wasted while we're choking. We consume and consume without any thought of why. Details, ideas, and concepts flow into our minds, then out again just as fast. Choking is like being on an information treadmill. We are rushing, even though we're not going anywhere. Life is a series of blurred impressions and half-formed thoughts.

Choking crowds out everything else. We can't consider changing our behavior or perspective when we're choking. Why? Because when we choke, we miss out on the opportunity to adapt and improve ourselves as a result of the rich sources of information to which we have access.

We are only a Google search away from starting to learn a new skill or finding a new job, but instead, we are watching compilation videos of cats[3] or Batdad.[4]

ANATOMY OF DISTRACTION

The information that keeps us choking is so ridiculous and over-the-top that we feel compelled to click. Here are a few examples, pulled randomly from real articles that I found online.

"Which 90s Cartoon Dog Are You?"[5]

"She Thought She Was Just Playing Super Mario, But Instead, He Was Proposing To Her!"[6]

"Inside the 'Shark Tank' Pitch That Ended With Kevin O'Leary Telling An Entrepreneur To 'Get The F— Out Of Here'"[7]

Is it any wonder that 660,000 Americans are using their phones while driving during peak traffic hours?[8] Or that surveys show 67 percent of us use phones at the dinner table, and 35 percent of us use them at church?[9] How about the fact that over 90 percent of us stare down at our phones even while we're walking?[10]

And this isn't just an American phenomenon. It's global. A Chinese city recently installed a "no cell phone" lane for people who want to walk without running into distracted citizens.[11]

Why is this such a problem?

UNHEALTHY INFORMATION

Humans do not respond well to an infinite supply of anything. This is the reason that obesity has become such a problem around the world, not just in America.[12] When we have too much food, our default is to eat every last bit of it. That's why obesity rates have *almost tripled* around the world since 1975.

Choosing quality over quantity is hard for us. Present someone with the choice between eating vegetables or cookies. What do they think that person would choose?

The cookies, of course. We will go for what's immediately more appealing without considering the implications of that single choice, or the habit we are reinforcing.

In this way, information is the same as food. We aren't wired to know when to stop. That means choking on all this newly available information is natural. We're curious creatures, and at some basic level, we want to see it all. We enjoy the mental stimulation, and the illusion that we're learning something new.

That's the tricky part. Choking often *feels* like we're doing something active when we are actually consuming mindlessly. That *feeling* of activity is what lets us stumble along with our heads down, thumbs a-blazing on our phones.

And what happens when you are using any computer that's connected to the internet? Distractions assault you with a vengeance as soon as you glance at it.

Unlocking your phone is not about you getting access to it. It's about the digital world getting access to you!

Personal computers—desktops, laptops, tablets, phones, watches, and more—do not function like our tools anymore. They are starting to control our behavior in some deep and troubling ways.

A DIGITAL DIET

Consider the sheer volume of information. One new book is put up on Amazon *every five* minutes.[13] Three-hundred hours of YouTube videos are uploaded per minute.[14] Six thousand tweets per second.[15] There is so much information out there. The scale of production is staggering. And so is the threat to you and me, yet somehow, we have to figure out how to deal with it.

Let's return to food for a minute. How do we address obesity? We try to teach people how to be healthy. We help people adopt the right mindset and behaviors. We want everyone to be able to manage their own weight. And if we have the means, we will probably find an expert to train us in the best practices of diet and exercise. That way we ensure that the habits stick.

The same straightforward logic applies to how we consume information. Instead of savoring high-quality

information—what we would call knowledge or wisdom—
we cram ourselves full of whatever junk is right in front
of our faces. What's worthy of consumption gets lost in
the tsunami of crap.

But it's so convenient! We jump from pin to post, or post
to article, or article to video, or video to thread. And then
back again.

We think we can handle this abundance, but we can't. It's
like trying to sip water out of a fire hose. We are taking
on way too much. When fun and appealing information
comes at you, sooner or later—and it will probably be
sooner—you're going to choke.

KNOWING IS HALF THE BATTLE

We need to understand how we process information to
truly understand choking. A better grasp of the situation
will help us take corrective steps to minimize the problem.
So, let's dive in!

All the information we consume falls on the spectrum of
comprehension. On one end, you have passive comprehension. On the other, active comprehension.

Passively comprehending means we consume information
without intending to process or act on it. It's just there,

so we let it wash over us. On the other hand, actively comprehending means we carefully consider the information and then—if appropriate—modify our mindset and/or behavior.

It's up to us whether we comprehend something passively or actively. Unfortunately, passive comprehension is intuitive. We are all great at mindless consumption. No training required! Where we struggle is carving out time to spend with the good stuff.

Active comprehension means wrestling with something—often for a long time on a deep level. Active comprehension requires focus. You are *marinating* in the information. And to do that, you need to be right there in the moment, fully present.

Being focused and purposeful is the hardest thing for us to do in this age of digital distraction. Few of us can break the spell of addictive information delivered directly to our eyeballs. So we choke instead. We consume without exercising judgment or connecting to a larger purpose.

When we choke, all information is experienced the same way, from pure gold to total rubbish. You're still looking at a screen. There are still words. There are still images. There are still videos. There is no obvious physical reason why you should be paying more attention to some information and not the rest.

Without any useful filters, we go for what's convenient. We want what feels good right now. Right now! *Right now!*

CHOKING 2.0

I've encountered this problem in my own life, of course. Witness my *Drunk History* story from the beginning of the chapter.

Choking, being completely overwhelmed with information flows, is the single biggest practical problem we face related to technology. It defines our relationship with almost everything invented since the iPhone came out in 2007, igniting the smartphone revolution.

There are now millions of businesses operating online that compete for our attention. They are constantly coming up with ways to keep us riveted and strung out on "free" content. It's no accident that YouTube modified their platform so another video loads automatically after the first one finishes.[16]

That's an example of infinite scroll, the ultimate choke point. You keep scrolling or thumbing down the page. It goes on forever. You could keep scrolling for the rest of your life...

As we'll see in later chapters, these digital intrusions are only going to get worse. The more sophisticated the technology, the better the design, and the more customized and seamless the advertising experience, the easier it will be for us to choke.

You thought the smartphone made it hard to get things done? Wait until you are plugging into a virtual reality bodysuit in a few years. Or when you are directly connected to the internet via nanobots in your brain. Even though it sounds like science fiction, these developments are already underway.

A BRAVE NEW WORLD

There are thousands of innovations happening right now that will make it even more critical to Reset our perspective and habits for the digital world. Each of them is a double-edged sword—sharp enough to be useful, but also sharp enough to be dangerous.

It's up to us to harness each wave of products and services. There is a near-infinite horizon of possibilities for us if we can just get started down the path of a purposeful life supported by the right mindset, habits, and structures.

That's how we can avoid physical obesity, and that's also how we're going to avoid mental obesity.

This is the challenge and opportunity of the digital world. Yes, we have to avoid distractions. And yes, these same technologies and companies can also be incredibly valuable to us. The difference is whether we Reset our mindset and daily habits.

If we Reset, we will be rewarded with a more meaningful, fulfilling, and impactful life. If we Reset, we will be able to find and absorb the best from the world's experts on any subject. If we Reset, we will be able to learn to cook a delicious meal, build a robot, negotiate a million-dollar deal, lose weight...anything! We will be in control of our own futures in a way that was impossible just a generation ago.

The only catch is that the process will be difficult. It takes time to learn how to adapt to the digital world. We need to Reset many fundamental aspects of our lives. Why? Because our default settings actually undermine our lives in important ways.

Just look at how we behave today. Adults in the US spend an average of five hours and thirty-one minutes consuming some kind of video content *each day*.[17] That was in 2015. Which direction do you think that number is headed?

This explosion of consumption extends across the world. British research group Ofcom tracks the amount of time people spend online every day. The total figure in 2005 was nine hours and fifty-four minutes. Ten years later, it more than doubled to twenty hours and thirty minutes.[18]

Our distracted and mindless behavior—choking is only the most obvious culprit of many—takes us away from doing what we want to be doing. All our normal excuses miss the point. It's not the lack of time, or the terrible boss, or the annoying friends, or the student loan debt.

It's the fact that we spent so much time choking instead of pursuing a purpose to which we choose to dedicate ourselves.

Starting to get the picture? Our current behavior isn't sustainable. What used to work has become the source of our problems. Now we are distracted, overworked, anxious, and disconnected from the people around us. That's what happens to us when we mindlessly repeat the behavior of previous generations. Things are changing too fast now. We need to update our thinking and our behavior.

MEET A CHOKER

My friend Andrew is a perfect example of how we easily get distracted in the digital world. He runs a mobile application development company in San Francisco, and he's made hundreds of apps in the last few years.

Andrew is a productive guy, but nowhere near maximizing his potential. If there was ever a guy who should avoid distractions, it's him. He can bring in a lot of money when he is on point. A good day for Andrew could be making $5,000!

This overwhelming profit incentive still doesn't stop him from choking. Andrew's worst enemy is Reddit. He is just four keystrokes away from being completely derailed. He hits Command + T to open a new tab, then types the letter R, and the Reddit URL automatically populates in the search bar. Then he hits Enter.

That takes what? Two seconds?

Once he's on Reddit, Andrew will waste at least an hour of scrolling through random fun facts about the internet. Maybe after that, he'll get back on task. Maybe.

Think of how different that is from the world just a few years ago. The good: Andrew can accomplish an incredible amount when he's firing on all cylinders. The bad: he could also read random threads on Reddit for an entire day. Literally.

Andrew is a smart guy with a good education. He triple-majored in philosophy, mathematics, and economics at a good college. But he still gets stuck choking. We all do!

Being smart or educated isn't the solution. Intelligence will not save you from choking. Neither will a PhD, nor computer programming skills, nor a million dollars. You are going to need a lot more if you want to be productive and fulfilled in your daily life. You must connect to your work, to the people you are impacting, and the life you aspire to live.

Changing your online behavior can seem incredibly difficult. It doesn't matter who you are or how much self-discipline you have. I still end up watching things like *Drunk History* occasionally, and I wrote this book!

There's no escaping the digital world. Our thumbs are itching to explore all the crazy and ridiculous stuff out there. *Scroll, scroll. Tap. Scroll, scroll, scroll, scroll. Tap.* We are hardwired with certain tendencies that make us susceptible to distractions, which we will learn about in later chapters.

The digital genie is out of the bottle. From now on, there will be an endless line of new innovations for us to figure out how to use. First, it was desktops and laptops, then phones. Now, it is watches and glasses. Soon it will be implants, and who knows after that. These products will keep coming. And you're fighting to keep yourself on track and be purposeful, to be the master of your own life.

Against some formidable opponents.

□—□—□

What to remember about "Choke":

- We spend a lot of our time online exposed to constant distractions.
- Choking occurs when we become overwhelmed with information.
- Advances in technology will make it easier every day for us to choke.
- We must develop habits to help us avoid choking.

Take three minutes to reflect on the following questions:

- How often do I get overwhelmed with information?
- During a typical day, when and where am I most likely to choke?
- What is my favorite source of mindless information?

If you want to spend five minutes learning more about choking, read *Addicted to Distraction* by Tony Schwartz.[19]

If you want to spend eight minutes learning more about choking, watch "We Are All Cyborgs Now,"[20] a TED Talk by Amber Case.

```
┌─────────────────────────────────────┐
│          C H A P T E R   T W O        │
└─────────────────────────────────────┘
                    │
┌─────────────────────────────────────┐
│                                       │
│         OLD SCHOOL                    │
│                                       │
└─────────────────────────────────────┘
```

OLD SCHOOL

W H O ' S   I N   C H A R G E ?

"The Times They Are A-Changin'"

—BOB DYLAN, AMERICAN MUSICIAN AND SONGWRITER

No matter how amazing the education, no one is prepared for the massive disruptions that we all face as the world transitions to digital. We are straddling the past and the future. One foot is in the world of long-distance calls (remember those?) and encyclopedias, while the other foot is in a new environment of Skype and Wikipedia.

This is a unique moment in history. We'll see in this and the next few chapters how a combination of forces—educational, social, and economic—are blending together in unexpected ways. The result? A massive opportunity for you and me if we can figure out how to Reset our mindset and habits.

And a life of anxiety and mindless consumption if we don't.

Let's run through a brief history of the world's transition from scattered farmers to workers in modern cities. This will help explain how we got here and why we are struggling to adapt to the digital world.

THE APPRENTICE

To begin, rewind the clock 1,500 years. Back in 500 AD, the average person didn't receive anything like a modern education. She probably wasn't literate. She probably couldn't write, except maybe her name. She knew almost nothing about the world outside the village where she was born. And that same village would likely be the place she died, as well.

Of course, she would have some informal training, mostly through her parents, maybe the local church, or the extended family. That's how she learned about her community's beliefs and values.

In terms of a job, folks in 500 AD had a tough choice. Either do what their parents did, or do what your parents did.

Young people would apprentice to their parents, or maybe someone in the village with a better job. In exchange, you did a decade or two of unpaid work, of course.

They're a farmer? You're a farmer. They're a merchant? You're a merchant. They're a blacksmith? You're a blacksmith.

And that's the men, who had it much better. Women in 500 AD had even fewer choices. They were basically forced into a domestic life. Hope you like—and survive—being pregnant, giving birth, and raising lots of children!

Sounds fantastic, doesn't it?

That system cranked along just fine for a long, long time. There was no compelling reason or opportunity to change it. And so, our daily lives looked the same as our grandparents' lives. And our own grandchildren still would be doing the same stuff a few generations later.

We have all read about these types of societies. There are textbooks with all kinds of pictures and stories about infant mortality, rampant disease, and constant violence. The world was Hobbesian: poor, nasty, brutish, and short.

But it's one thing to flash across this era in a few short paragraphs. *Experiencing* this kind of world would blow our minds! Until we see it for ourselves, we cannot imagine how different life is for someone in a traditional, pre-industrial society.

HERDING SHEEP

I actually came face-to-face with a society that operated similar to this model. I met real-life shepherds in Afghanistan when I was deployed there as a Marine between 2010 and 2011. No kidding, shepherds. As in, their job was to move around sheep without losing any of them. They wore robes and held crooked staffs.

I can only describe them as "biblical."

The guys I met were shepherds because their fathers were shepherds. And their fathers were shepherds because their grandfathers were shepherds. And they were teaching their sons to do the same thing. What other option did they have?

That agrarian world couldn't exist forever except in places like Afghanistan, which ranks in the bottom 5 percent of the UN's Human Development Index.[1] Much of that country—particularly the southern tribal areas—is stuck in the past. Not exactly something to which we should be aspiring.

After spending seven months deployed in Afghanistan, I returned home to Silicon Valley. From the Flintstones to the Jetsons. And in the process, I experienced just how quickly and violently we are tearing ourselves away from very old, very humble beginnings.

Within three months of coming home from war, I was working at Singularity University.[2] This organization—backed by organizations like Google and NASA—is tackling humanity's biggest challenges with rapidly advancing technologies. Everyone is an engineer, entrepreneur, or both. They are looking at areas such as artificial intelligence, mining asteroids, and genetically engineering us to be free from disease, environmental disaster, and aging.

Meanwhile, my shepherd friend is still herding his sheep.

Singularity University showed me just how fast the world is changing. I also discovered that this rapid evolution is directed by a tiny group of people. They are the ones driving these changes through a particular breed of entrepreneurship. We'll learn a lot more about them in Chapter Six.

So here we all are, sandwiched between the Flintstones and the Jetsons. How the heck did we get to this point?

The current pace of innovation obviously didn't happen overnight. Technological progress has been building momentum for several thousand years. It is powered by the efforts of millions of people. People discover new things. People turn those discoveries into useful stuff. People take that useful stuff and discover *even more* new things. The cycle feeds back into itself. The wheel spins faster, and faster, and faster...

This cycle of technological innovation works better when we live close to each other. It turns out that population density is the single biggest predictor of innovation and progress. Why? Because people are at their best when they are working together, and it's much easier to work together when everyone is stuck in one place.*

In other words, the progress from Flintstones to Jetsons is driven by people. And people work better when we are packed together. So the history of human progress should also be the history of people gathering together.

And it is. As of 2010, more than half of us live in cities now. That's a huge migration away from traditional farming societies.³ But this trend started a long time ago. Let's

---

* It's way more complicated than that. Read Ramez Naam's *The Infinite Resource* to understand more about population density, creativity, and innovation: http://www.amazon.com/ The-Infinite-Resource-Finite-Planet/dp/161168255X.

take another backward look at human history from the perspective of innovation, rather than lifestyle.

People started clustering in villages as we developed more productive agricultural systems thousands of years ago. More productivity meant more food. More food meant more people. And we like hanging out together, so more and more of us made the switch from nomads to settlers. More people pooling in one place.

Villages slowly grew into towns. Towns slowly grew into cities. And these cities are the environments where new ideas—the seeds of innovation—thrive.

Art, drama, and literature are the most visible parts of urban culture, but they aren't the real story. Advances in science and technology are the fundamental game-changers. One invention can be used to create many other inventions. And one theory can be used to explain all kinds of phenomena in the world.

Our lives are defined by this explosive combination of new ways of thinking and practical inventions. These two forces started in the cities and spread outward from there. These islands of innovation were transforming the world.

The first major wave with a lasting global impact was the Industrial Revolution. Starting in the late eighteenth century, this powerful movement swept country after country into the modern age.* In just a few generations, farming economies across the UK, Europe, and the US awkwardly morphed into industrial economies. That's lightning quick by the standards of a human civilization.

A BRAVE NEW JOB

The Industrial Revolution[4] placed an incredible burden on the population. People needed to do new kinds of work. Unlike previous generations, young workers could not rely on their parents. Suddenly, there were new options: do I stay here at the farm or try my luck in the city?

People now had choices that had never existed before. Millions of us confront this choice every year, primarily in rural areas.

The choice isn't exactly a great one. Yes, farming is unpredictable and back-breaking. But industrial work is dirty, dangerous, and boring. Working in factories meant doing repetitive tasks that we don't naturally enjoy doing. Owners of these new industrial businesses therefore had a problem. They had to figure out a way to train kids to perform the work that adults were unwilling or unable to do.

---

*   A great and entertaining summary of the industrial revolution: https://www.youtube.com/watch?v=zhL5DCizj5c

In other words, companies needed a way to tap into a pipeline of people who would be able to work in boring, repetitive environments with disciplined taskmasters.

And so the modern school is born.

Modern schools are a logical response to the needs of the businesses that fueled the Industrial Revolution. These were the companies who were displacing farming as the primary supplier of jobs. The need for workers provided a clear economic rationale for modern schools. After all, schools were the source of the trained workers. That's an important reason why schools were established more quickly in the New England states.[5] These states were industrializing quickly, so they needed the workers. Of course, there are other reasons for the spread of public education, but the powerful financial incentives made it certain that state-sponsored, industrial schooling quickly became the standard.

Obviously, we don't live in an industrial economy anymore. If you look at employment in the United States over the twentieth century, you can see a huge shift to the service sector.[6] Over 80 percent of us now work in fields like nursing, truck driving, consulting, banking, and restaurants.[7]

Even while we were industrializing, the seeds were being sown for the next wave: the service economy. No country had the chance to catch their breath before being destabilized yet again. The cycle of innovation only speeds up, remember?

THE NEXT BIG SHIFT

The service economy was similar enough to the industrial economy to temporarily mask some massive changes going on. As in the industrial economy, people were finding stable, long-term employment working for companies. They were locked into a career once they managed to get hired. Hierarchy, repetition, and stability were still the norm in the workplace. Everything revolved around the *job*.

The economy is still changing rapidly, though. Progress didn't stop a few decades ago. In fact, it's speeding up! These changes are obvious when we look at the nature of the work people are doing. Consider the emergence of an entirely new type of worker: the dependent contractor.[8] It's not yet a legal category, but the government is looking carefully at how on-demand workers—Uber drivers, for example—should be treated by companies.*

It's hard enough to slap a label on this new era, let alone understand how our individual roles are changing. John Howkins tried to popularize the phrase "creative econ-

---

*   As of this writing in April 2018.

omy",[9] though it never caught on.[10] That's a shame because it does a great job of distilling the essence of our new role in the world. You and I will need to be creatively engaged to be successful. We are shifting away from the *job* you have to the *value* you create for others.

The creative economy is the financial side of the digital world. It operates by a completely different set of rules than a society dominated by the service sector, the industrial sector, or the agricultural sector. And that is the point of this chapter: we were trained in the old school while the world was changing right under our feet!

NEW RULES

Creativity is about purpose, about inspiration, and about people. We need to create value for others in new and exciting ways, then share that value far and wide. This creative mindset is a totally new way of seeing the world. You'll learn more about the specifics of this mindset in Chapters Seven through Nine.

We are not prepared to thrive in this environment, though. And why not? Because the incentives and structures in our daily lives are shifting in fundamental ways. You must be able to Reset your mindset and daily rituals if you are going to thrive in the creative economy, and in the digital world.

To quote an early *Spiderman* comic, "In this world, with great power there must also come—great responsibility!"[11] This has never been more true for us. We are being freed from the constraints that defined the human condition since we emerged at the top of the food chain. But at the same time, more and more information is popping up all over the place. These distractions are tearing us away from our creative, fulfilling pursuits.

Think back to the shepherd. He had one choice: do what his father did. Then the industrial society opened up a few choices, such as factory worker. The service sector quickly followed, adding opportunities in a variety of other fields. But the digital world took this to the next level with the creative economy. Now anyone can do anything, or so it seems.

These changes are both a gift and a curse. On the one hand, we can basically determine our own life path. It's impossible to imagine just how different life is for us to have that level of freedom. Yet everything we learn in childhood and adolescence presumes that we should already know the work we're supposed to be doing.

Identifying and pursuing your goals through purposeful daily work is left as an afterthought. But it's not an afterthought at all! It's actually the most critical skill that we need to develop in the digital world.

The old, stable world is gone. We just don't want to acknowledge it. The temptation is to bury our heads in the sand and our thumbs on our screens. We hope that someone figures out a way for us to have a high-paying job and plenty of time for family and friends.

Maybe there's an app for that...

Deep down, we know there is no quick and easy solution. The problems of our generation require thoughtful action over the long term. Think about what you read in the news every day. Resurgent populism. Democracy under attack. Over a *trillion* dollars in student loan debt.[12] Widening inequality.[13] A shrinking middle-class.[14] Increasing debt.[15]

It should be clear to everyone that we need new organization, structures, and mindsets to handle the rapid pace of change that defines the twenty-first century.

But that's not what is happening. Most of us are being set up to fail based on nothing but societal momentum. We grew up in a system that was based on the scarcity of information and rewards for conformity.

SCHOOL FOR HAMSTERS

Consider a typical education. The teacher is the gatekeeper. He or she controls the resources, and the students have no other way of getting the information. We receive our homework like little food pellets. One at a time, perfectly packaged, and easy to consume. Just follow the steps and we'll get our reward.

Where's the creativity or fulfillment in that?

This ridiculous process is basically the same in college as it is in kindergarten. And we follow it because it earns us A's and smiley-face stickers. Study, study, study. Don't ask why. Just pass the test and then forget everything you just learned because there is another pointless test coming up in a few weeks.

That will not cut it anymore. We can't just check the boxes.

Research into creativity in schools scares me, especially because I'm one of the products of this educational Play-Doh factory. Ninety-five percent of second graders think they are creative, but that statistic flips entirely by the time they are seniors in high school, when only 5 percent identify as creative.[16] And this is what's happening at a time when creativity is needed more than ever!

Aside from basic literacy and social skills, traditional education is useless—even counterproductive—in the digital world. Our brains are terrible at information storage and retrieval compared to computers. So why bother using your brain like a crappy version of a computer? Computers do these repetitive tasks better than us already, and the gap is growing.[17] The digital world is quickly pulling away from the old human-centered systems. And we need to adapt or risk a life of constant distractions and unfulfilled work.

TO WORK OR NOT TO WORK

Traditional jobs are still out there, of course. They aren't going away overnight. The number-one job in the state of California, believe it or not, is truck driver. In the United States, more people drive trucks than any other job. In fact, truck driver is the number-one job in thirty-one out of fifty states![18] But sooner or later that's going to change because people tend to get tired and make mistakes. We crash our cars, in other words. In fact, we lose tens of thousands of lives each year in the United States from automotive accidents due to human error.[19]

Eventually computers will not crash cars. Maybe not in 2025 or 2035, but eventually. Where does that leave us? What does it mean that we won't have to drive ourselves anymore? What the heck will all those millions of people do?

The answer may surprise you. It cuts to the heart of the creative economy, and the challenge we face during these periods of societal transition.

One hundred years ago, when cars were just hitting the mass market, horses were the dominant form of transportation. "Horse pollution" was the main topic of conversation at the world's first urban planning conference in 1898.[20] A New York City public health official claimed that 20,000 people died each year from the unsanitary conditions resulting from so many horses.[21]

People had a hard time imagining life without horses. But when it turned out that cars were faster and more reliable, everyone made the switch in a relatively short period of time. The percentage of households owning a car went from under 10 percent to over 60 percent in barely fifteen years![22]

Horses couldn't learn new skills, so they weren't able to adapt. They became sideshows. Now, the only time most of us see a horse racing is in the Kentucky Derby or pulling a carriage in Central Park.

Ready to be uncomfortable? Let's return to today, take out the word "horses," replace it with "humans," and reconsider the situation. Why won't we become sideshows, too? Computers are performing more and more tasks. Things we used to think were off-limits. Things only people could do. This leads us to an uncomfortable question. Will humans be necessary in the digital world once it fully matures?

I am optimistic. We probably will be necessary in the digital world, but it won't happen automatically. If you and I have jobs in twenty years, it won't be because we're good at repetitive tasks like driving a truck.

Our advantage over horses is that we are very good at creatively solving important problems. We solve problems in our own lives and in the lives of others. We discover new areas to explore, then find innovative ways to accomplish meaningful goals within them. We create value and we recognize where value is created by others. We anticipate what people in our society want and need, and then we create products and services to fulfill those needs.

RE-EDUCATION

I was a product of a public school system when there still was a relatively good fit between what we learned and what was needed in the economy. In 2000, when I graduated high school, there was let's say, a 75 percent fit.* I was adequately prepared for a variety of work environments.

When someone graduates now, the fit between student abilities and economic needs is more like 25 percent. Probably less.

Almost none of the information "learned" by a student

---

* These percentages are like business school graphs: not exact figures but important conceptually.

is retained. More importantly, the habits and mindset being taught to kids will hurt them once they enter the workforce. The helpful stuff is really the social skills: being around different types of kids, sharing with others, group activities, playing sports, and so on.

The idea that kids are being educated in any meaningful way is a complete illusion. The test scores, the report cards, and the parent-teacher meetings only prop up the illusion. Being a good student does not mean you're smarter than anybody else. It just means you have a specific set of skills and a mindset that lets you accomplish certain kinds of tasks. You're a good fit for that specific system. But that system is an artificial construct with little predictive power once you leave the classroom.

Researchers discovered something counterintuitive when they looked at grades and how they affected professional achievement. Grades have almost no impact on how well you do after school.[23] And here's another interesting finding that shouldn't surprise you by now: studies from before 1950 showed a much larger benefit. GPA matters less today, not more! And soon, the positive effect will disappear entirely.

The digital world doesn't want hamsters. It wants passionate creatives.

If you are not a good student naturally, that means you

aren't naturally interested in certain behaviors. Sitting still, doing the same thing over and over, waiting patiently, following instructions without questioning, *et cetera*. Basically, that means you wouldn't be a good factory worker.

The current system costs us in many ways. I am already thinking about how these changes apply to my children. I don't want them to be good students in the sense of feeling comfortable sitting in a classroom for over a decade, except for summer breaks that are all full of organized activities. That steady drip-drip-drip education will be completely out of place once they enter real life.

I don't want them to become shepherds or factory workers. I want them to be creatives with a focus on developing products and services that other people find valuable.

Self-directed passion and focus is the bedrock of the creative economy. Whether you're an Uber driver or the CEO of a giant company, you need to figure out how to be part of that value-based process in some important way.

That is the task of everyone in the digital world: to figure out creative ways to become valuable to others through meaningful work every day. If you use your brain as a storage space, you will soon be as useless as horses are today. Instead, you want to use your brain to be useful, to progress toward important goals, to improve your behavior, and to have a positive impact on the world.

If you're not one of the Jetsons, you're probably one of the Flintstones.

▣—▣—▣

What to remember about "Old School":

- The school system emerged to fill the needs of an industrial society.
- Hierarchy and repetition used to be fundamental elements of our work lives.
- Computers do most of the repetitive work, so our economy is rewarding independence and creativity.
- We need to reprogram ourselves to focus on this type of creative work.

Take three minutes to reflect on the following questions:

- What habits from school do you still use today?
- Which of these may be holding you back?
- What new skills could make you more useful to others?

If you want to spend five minutes learning more about our educational system, read "Gus the Truck: A Metaphor for an Outdated Education System"[24] by Tony Lewis and Ann Anderson.

If you want to spend seven minutes learning more about changes in the workforce, read "The Automation Revolution and the Rise of the Creative Economy"[25] by Aidan Cunniffe.

If you want to spend twenty minutes learning more about our educational system, watch "Do Schools Kills Creativity?"[26] a TED Talk by Sir Ken Robinson.

CHAPTER THREE

PHOTOSHOPPING

WHY DO I FEEL LIKE I'M MISSING OUT ON LIFE?

"I am an old man and have known a great many troubles, but most of them never happened."

—ATTRIBUTED TO MARK TWAIN, AMERICAN AUTHOR

Our inadequate education is only one part of the mismatch between us and our environment. The digital world is operating in one way, while you and I are rooted in an older system with very different rules.

Nowhere is this dynamic more powerful than the way we interact with other people. Human beings are social animals, and this can be twisted to our disadvantage. In fact, that is happening right now. Our online behavior is creating an echo chamber of depression.

My wife and I were recently at a party where we were both bored out of our minds. Everything about this party sucked: the music, the people, the food, everything. So what did we do? Leave? Of course not! We took a great picture of us smiling and put it up on Instagram.

The rest of this story should sound familiar. My wife's friends see the picture and think we are having a great time. More importantly, they are convinced we are having a better time *than them.*

Cue the destructive self-talk: "Look at them, having so much fun. She looks so good. And he's smiling so nicely. I bet they are going someplace awesome after that, too. Maybe I should have gone to that other party instead. Everyone around here looks so bored." And on and on and on.

Of course, they don't understand that we took this picture because we were bored. Their emotions are aroused based on one digitally retouched picture with no context! That's the point. No one *ever* sees the whole story online. Why? Because we only show each other what we want to show.

Everyone does this. You, me, everyone. We put up some idealized slices of our lives, which then become the standard by which others judge themselves. We exaggerate our own highs, and that exaggerates the lows of everyone else.

Our online communities are constantly infecting us with unrealistic impressions of the world around us. Let's call this phenomenon photoshopping.

MISMATCH

This self-destructive behavior stems from new tools that we haven't yet learned how to use properly. Humans can invent things much faster than we can learn to use things. Our biology doesn't update like a computer.

You and I make decisions using the same brain that our ancestors had thousands of years ago. And unfortunately, our environment is changing a lot faster than any single individual's ability to adapt.

Why is this a problem? Because our expectations about life—rooted in legacy culture—no longer correspond to reality. These expectations affect our behavior in thousands of tiny ways every day. And those mismatched interactions cause everyone to suffer needlessly.

THE ORIGINAL SOCIAL NETWORK

Human beings are inherently social. We are built to care

about our family and friends. That instinct helps us survive by working in groups to accomplish goals that are impossible for individuals.

Collaboration in tribes and other small communities—relying on each other to accomplish common goals—has worked out very well for us as a species.[1] It even seems to be reflected in the structure of our brains and the natural size limits of our tribal communities.[2]

While these hardwired social inclinations have been useful for us, they only make sense in the physical world. There is a limit to the number of people we can interact with at one time and over the course of a lifetime.

Our extended family and tribal networks used to number dozens, maybe hundreds of members. We knew them for long periods of time. And we knew them within the context of our daily lives. Compare that to the reality most of us experience in an urban environment. It is estimated that the average city-dweller will meet at least 80,000 people during the course of his or her life.[3]

How many of our urban neighbors will you and I ever really know? Almost none. These random people are blurry, anonymous shapes that flicker in and out of our lives. And yet, we are still hardwired to care about them.

That's why you don't make eye contact with people when you walk down the street. You don't *want* to care, and eye contact triggers that natural human tendency to connect.

PLUGGED IN, TUNED OUT

The digital world takes our social experiences to a whole new level. Now we are interacting with a wide range of people in short bursts in a variety of online environments. If 80,000 random city-dwellers sounded like a big number of chance encounters, imagine how many more people you will bump into on Facebook, Twitter, Instagram, LinkedIn, and Snapchat!

Life on social media is a stream of fleeting impressions. Each one is a potential source of anxiety for our mal-adapted brains. We are bombarded by carefully curated glimpses of events and relationships. These are ghost images. Real but not tangible.

Every word, image, and video we see has been put through a series of filters, metaphorically and literally. Each post and update is an attempt by someone else to inch up the digital hierarchy. Our social instincts are being twisted into an endless series of humble brags, those little "look at me!" posts you see all the time.* We are all looking for

---

* The best definition of "humble brag" is on Urban Dictionary: https://www.urbandictionary. com/define.php?term=humblebrag

other people to validate us, an urge that cannot be fully satisfied. So, we post over and over again. It's a compulsion.

We're starting to get the first scientific studies showing us the consequences of heavy social media use.[4] Depression, poor body image, and other kinds of negative behaviors are emerging in this hyper-connected world that was grafted onto our lives in barely a decade.[5]

The lack of control over this phenomenon is frightening. We are all convinced that being connected has somehow made our lives better, but there is not much evidence to support that fact. We might *feel* more connected, but we are confusing connection with entertaining distractions. Our natural desire for friendship and community is driving us to the very thing that is isolating us!

Kids are the worst affected, since they adopt these technologies first and most intensely. Experts have speculated about a wide variety of effects, ranging from obesity to developmental disorders.[6],[7] The latest generation is growing up with this hyper-connectedness integrated into every aspect of their lives. Over 90 percent of them use social media every day.[8]

Few of us are exempt from the influences of these (still new) online communities. After all, most of us also use social media. This new class of social interaction dominates our daily life. Or at least it did for 65 percent of us in 2015, compared to 7 percent in 2005.[9] That's a ninefold increase in ten years!

Think about everything you do through social media. We get information, especially breaking news, from social media.[10] We begin relationships through social media.[11] We rely on social media for parenting advice and social support.[12] We filter ourselves because of social media and concern about the popularity of our beliefs or opinions.[13] We turn to social media when we're bored. And we navigate all the various options simultaneously, overloading ourselves with social signals.[14] All these changes to our daily lives are based on something that didn't even exist twenty years ago!

This new type of obsessive online behavior is a double-edged sword for the same reasons as any other part of the digital world. It can be great when we consciously control our exposure and behavior, but that is not how most of us use social media. Instead, it is often an obstacle to a fulfilling life.

We must use the tool, not be used by it. If we don't start curating our exposure to social media, we will be overwhelmed by a tsunami of social signals every day.

Of course, the human desire for social interaction is a

beautiful thing. Our empathy explains the most remarkable kinds of selfless behavior. We don't want to get rid of that. We want to harness it, which is precisely what we will discuss later on.

STRANGER DANGER

Our mismatched social instincts betray us in another dangerous way: we overestimate danger in the world around us. This tendency makes sense in some ways. As animals, we are conditioned to avoid danger, however possible. We respond to perceived threats with a knee-jerk emotional reaction. We are built to believe there are threats out there, and we should be afraid of them.

Consider the articles that get shared online. How many are positive versus negative? Which ones do we tend to share? Which ones go viral? The outrageous and grotesque events, of course.[15] The "I can't believe it!" events. And this has a devastating impact on us, whether or not we realize it. All these terrible images and stories blend together into a constant sense of fear. A manufactured fear. This paralyzing dynamic darkens our view of the world.

But perception is not reality.

Despite what you would think from the constant stream of online news, the American society is safer today than it's ever been. Child mortality rates are about 50 percent of the 1990 levels, which is a record low.[16] Missing children reports are down 40 percent since 1993.[17] The number of kids hit and killed by cars is down by more than 70 percent since 1993.[18] And it's not just children who are safer. We all are. The rates of murder, armed robbery, aggravated assault, and property crime are all at their lowest levels in history![19]

Do you feel twice as safe as you did twenty years ago? Of course not. The opposite is probably true. We are saturated with fear-based media for one reason: we pay attention to it. As everyone knows, "if it bleeds, it leads." But this phrase takes on a whole new meaning in the hyperconnected digital world where anything, credible or not, can feed into our sense of the world.

FEAR NOT

Fear has a catastrophic effect on our well-being. Fear holds us back from building and deepening the authentic relationships we crave as humans. We will overestimate our odds of becoming a victim, perceive our communities as unsafe, and the view the whole world as dangerous.[20]

It's like pouring acid on our own souls.

This kind of manufactured fear is still photoshopping, but

it's photoshopping in a much more insidious way. Instead of airbrushing that model's face on the latest cover of *Vogue*, we are letting digital media put negative filters on the world beyond our front door.

"Why go out into a sea of lunatics?" we ask ourselves. And we're only half-kidding. Blinded by fake dangers, we cannot see the opportunities in front of us. We shift our gaze from goals and aspirations to threats and dangers. And our natural response is to stay inside, to check out of life.

Neither of these distorted perspectives—jealousy or fear—will take us in the right direction. We will never be fulfilled by chasing after illusions of success or filtered party pictures on Instagram. And we will never be safe by running away from manufactured dangers that are crammed down our throats every day.

Our biology and our technology are not meshing well. Someone out there is making things much harder on us, spoiling the promise of the digital world.

□—□—□

What to remember about "Photoshopping":

- We are experiencing a distorted reality every day.

- Other people make their lives seem way better than they are.
- The media makes the world seem way worse than it is.
- The false highs and lows rob us of energy and optimism.

Take three minutes to reflect on the following questions:

- How much time do I spend on social media?
- Do I ever freak out as a result of things my friends post?
- Am I constantly worried about things I read about in media reports?

If you want to spend seven minutes learning more about photoshopping, read "5 Things the Media Does to Manufacture Outrage" by Parker Molloy.

If you want to spend twelve minutes learning more about photoshopping, watch "Life in the 'Digital Now,'"[21] a TED Talk by Abha Dawesar.

If you want to spend thirty minutes learning more about photoshopping, read "Taming the Mammoth: Why You Should Stop Caring What Other People Think"[22] by Tim Urban.

CHAPTER FOUR

MADDER MEN

WHO IS PAYING FOR THE INTERNET?

"Someone once said, 'Follow the Money'
and that is what it is all about."

—MURRAY WALKER, BRITISH JOURNALIST AND COMMENTATOR

Why do I feel so addicted to my screens? What is driving the rapid growth of social media and the larger digital world? How are technology companies making huge piles of cash?

It may not seem like it, but these three questions are all directly related. And asking these questions is the last step to understanding the world in which we now live. The surprising answers will help us understand why we are being betrayed by our educational system, social impulses, and consumer technologies.

In each case, the gigantic disconnect between expectations and reality comes down to one thing: money.

The digital world has humble beginnings, believe it or not. This global experiment began as a cluster of government-funded research networks.[1] Some really smart government scientists in the US and Europe needed to talk to one another across a variety of networks, and they were worried about losing connections if the telephone system went down. Their solution was to build a common system for all their computer networks. That's where the word "internet" comes from: inter-network.

Because the initial goal was helping highly technical researchers share information, there was no profit motive. All the money came from governments, meaning the early internet was paid for by American and European taxpayers.

But very quickly, companies saw a huge business opportunity with the internet. Imagine how much money you could make when your business could instantly communicate across the world with all its customers, suppliers, and partners! This was a huge opportunity for fast-moving businesses and visionary entrepreneurs. A few pioneering companies started lobbying governments for access, and eventually got the rules changed so they could participate.[2] That kicked off the era of the profit-driven internet, where we still are today.

This point is critical to understand. The expansion of the internet—and the birth of the digital world—is fueled by the quest for profit. Companies use the internet to make money.

Surprise!

YOU ARE THE PRODUCT

Think about the main websites and apps we use. Facebook (which includes Instagram), Twitter, Alphabet (which includes Google, Gmail, YouTube, *et cetera*), and Snapchat (for the younger crowd). These companies are the ones we go to more frequently than any others. Have you ever wondered how they make money? What the heck does anyone pay them for?

The answer is advertising. Advertising, advertising, and more advertising! Look at their quarterly financial results if you don't believe me. We may think these companies are technology companies, but the numbers tell a different story.

Alphabet made about $31 billion from January to March

2018, and almost $27 billion of that was from advertising![3] That's about 87 percent of their revenue. Facebook made about $12 billion in the same three-month period.[4] Guess how much of it was advertising—$11.8 billion, or 98 percent![5] Unfortunately, Snapchat doesn't give details about how much of its $285 million from October to December 2017 is from advertising.[6] And Twitter? In the January to March 2018 window, In the Janu$575 million out of $664 million came from advertising.[7] That's 86 percent profit from advertising, which is the lowest of the bunch!

All the other crazy stuff that comes out of the giant technology companies—the slick phones, the self-driving cars, the virtual reality, the (sort of) free global broadband network—is funded by advertising.* They can only do all the sexy stuff because they are selling advertising to other companies.

TIME IS MONEY

Advertising is business-speak, so we need to clear up the language. It means charging one person money to let them try to get the attention of someone else. Google does this through their search engine, while Facebook and Twitter do it through social media.

---

*   The "free" internet story is particularly interesting: http://www.thedailybeast.com/articles/2016/02/09/india-rejects-facebook-s-free-internet.html

Businesses have both customers and products. Two different groups: one that pays, and another that is the reason for the payment. Guess which one you are?

You are the product. Surprise again!

You are the reason that companies give money to Google, Facebook, Twitter, whoever. What you have is time. And companies are the customers for these big tech companies. These companies want you to spend your time buying their stuff. So, they will give money to Google, or Facebook, or whoever for the chance to distract you from whatever you are doing to go buy their stuff.

Does this make sense? People go to Taco Bell to buy burritos. People go to Foot Locker to buy shoes. Companies go to Google to buy you. More specifically, your attention.

So even though you think Google is made for you, it's not. You can benefit from using Google—I know I do—but that doesn't mean it's made for you. You are the product, all packaged up and ready to be sold to the highest bidder. The companies are the real customers. They have the money. They pay for the privilege of distracting you from what you want to do.

The top three websites in the US—Google, Facebook, You-Tube—all make money by selling you stuff via advertising.[8]

And yet, these same websites are amazing tools when you approach them with a clear purpose.

That sums up the challenge and opportunity of the digital world. We can accomplish great things *if* we can stay on track. And that's a pretty big *if*. The internet can be only one thing at a time: an infinitely powerful tool, or a gateway drug to endless distraction. It's up to you to change your mindset and daily behavior so you are using the digital world and not being used by it.

Which is why you're reading this, right?

PRICE OF FREEDOM

These technology companies—which are really advertising companies—have lots of customers, each one with tons of cash. They all want a piece of you. And they've stacked the deck in their favor. They are like the casino and you're a gambler. What's the expression?

The house always wins.

The technology companies are the ones paying for everything. And that money comes almost exclusively from advertising. Think back to the questions from the beginning of the chapter. How did you think the drastic expansion of the internet and digital connectivity was funded?

We've been misled by the surface of the digital world. Our primary exposure comes through social media and email, which are "free." We don't pay for a lot of the products and services we use online. But that isn't really true. They are "free" to us because we are the product, not the customers. Someone is still paying for the whole thing.

The rules didn't change for technology companies. Every business needs to make money. There are no exceptions. Now let's walk through the entire process to make sure we understand exactly how this works. Understanding the flow of money is critical.

CLICKBAIT

Nobody goes to Google to look at the ads, right? You go to Google to search for something, and along with the results, you get the ads that are subtly sprinkled in. If you click an ad, Google gets a few pennies (and sometimes much more) from the company that put up that ad. Every single time anyone clicks on any ad, someone somewhere is getting paid. And Google processes over 5.8 billion searches *per day*.[9]

The same financial logic holds true for the most popular websites. Eventually, they all need to find a way to make money off the people who visit them. These companies reel in billions of dollars every year with advertising. That means they are making fortunes by distracting you.

You might be online to look at a notification, search for something, check up on a friend, or read the latest news. But the company knows a whole lot about you, too. They can take data from your profile and combine it with other information to make a compelling sale. They can target you because they "know" a lot about who you are from your behavior history online.

In other words, these companies sell us, a few seconds at a time.

THE AUCTION BLOCK

If the bidding process took place in the real world, it would sound something like this.

"Hey, everyone! Gather around, please. Check out this delightful twenty-seven-year-old Asian-American woman who lives in the greater Austin area."

"She has a job as a marketing executive making between $65,000 and $70,000. She recently updated her relationship status to 'engaged.'"

"Let's start the bidding at $0.45 for an ad! Do I have $0.45? I have $0.45, thank you to the local gym."

"Do I have $0.50? I have $0.50, thank you to the jewelry store."

"Do I have $0.55? I have $0.55, thank you to the wedding planner."

"Do I have $0.60? Going once. Going twice. Sold for $0.55 to the wedding planner!"

This whole process takes less than a second. Thousands of companies have software that lets them bid automatically based on complex formulas. They are trying to guess what your attention is worth, based on the expected value of your purchases and the probability that you will buy something. That's how the process works.

US VERSUS THEM

The digital world keeps you from pursuing your own agenda by grabbing your attention. It wants you to choke. Not because the system is evil or anything like that. The digital world wants you to choke because choking pays the bills.

The more eyeballs that see each ad, the more people click on the ads. The more people who click on the ads, the more dollars go into the company's pockets.

Advertising—I mean, technology—companies have armies of digital marketers. Almost 250,000 of them in the United States alone.[10] They are using software to build systems that compete for our attention every second we are connected. They study us. What we like, where we live, who we connect with, and what we do. The more they know about you and me, the more addictive they can make the things that are offered to us.

Unlike you and me, the digital advertising machine never sleeps. Companies have already developed programs that run themselves; the ultimate set-it-and-forget-it. You are worth that much to these companies. That little check they collect every time you see an ad eventually adds up to billions of dollars in profits. The total revenue for digital advertising will soon top $200 *billion* dollars per year.[11] And think about the huge increase in screen time that we discussed in Chapter Two. Imagine how much that number will grow as more and more people join the digital world, and we get more and more addicted to it.

Ka. Ching.

Please don't misunderstand me. There is nothing wrong with profit. The problem we all face is that profit for these companies comes from our attention. They are selling their customers the chance to distract you from what you want to do. And they've barely gotten started. Soon, they'll be harnessing augmented reality, virtual reality, the Internet of Things, artificial intelligence, and the next thing after that.

Advertisers will be right there with you, ready to indulge you in the slightest whim, twenty-four-hours a day, seven days a week, 365 days a year. Forever.

GUT CHECK

It's time for the unvarnished truth. We are unprepared for the world in which we live, a digital world where we are the product being packaged and sold. We haven't been educated or trained for this always-on environment that is full of distractions. Some of us aren't even aware of what's happening.

For millions of people, there's a real possibility they will get stuck choking for the rest of their lives. It doesn't matter how old they are: twenty-five, fifty, seventy-five, or ten. They will be so distracted so much of the time that they will never accomplish any substantial goals. Many will never even figure out what their goals actually are.

Those who get stuck choking will have an unremarkable life. These unlucky souls will make a few half-hearted attempts to do something outside the norm. But these efforts won't last long.

The sad truth is some people will grow too comfortable with distractions. Distractions fit so easily into our lives. Distractions don't ask us to do anything different. All we need to give up is our attention. For the rest of our lives. That's why all these huge technology companies build products to be so addictive. They want us constantly coming back for more and more. That's their business model!

Stay distracted until you die. That is becoming the game plan for anyone who doesn't take control of his or her life. Just like Andrew's Reddit addiction from Chapter One, we can waste time online even though we know how deeply it affects our personal and professional lives.

But that's not your future, not if you are reading this. You are preparing to get engaged, to grapple with tough questions, to change your mindset, to take action, and to help others wake up, too. The rewards for our hard work have never been greater. We can build the life we want in the same digital world that threatens to overwhelm and incapacitate us.

The question is, "Do you want it bad enough?"

□—□—□

What to remember about "Madder Men":

- The expansion of the internet is funded by digital advertising.
- The most popular websites sell you stuff; that's why they are "free."
- We are not prepared to function effectively in this environment.

Take three minutes to reflect on the following questions:

- How many times per week do I buy things online?
- How often do I click ads when I'm online?
- If every click cost someone a dollar, how much money would I make for other people on the average day?

If you want to spend one minute investigating Twitter's business model, watch "How Twitter Makes Money."[12]

If you want to spend two minutes investigating Google's business model, watch "How Does Google Make Money?"[13]

If you want to spend seven minutes investigating Facebook's business model, watch "How Does Facebook Make Money?"[14]

If you want to spend three hours learning more about digital marketing, read *Trust Me, I'm Lying: Confessions of a Media Manipulator* by Ryan Holiday.[15]

PART II

THE INSPIRATION

CHAPTER FIVE

RESET

HOW BADLY DO I REALLY WANT TO CHANGE?

"Sometimes when you're overwhelmed by a situation—when you're in the darkest of darkness— that's when your priorities are reordered."

—PHOEBE SNOW, AMERICAN SINGER AND SONGWRITER

You and I are exploring some deep questions that are unique to life in the emerging digital world. How do we avoid the infinite distractions flying at us from every direction? How can we motivate ourselves without burning out in a hyperconnected society? How do we feel good about our lives when everyone else seems to be doing better than us?

This can seem overwhelming, but it doesn't have to be. Effectively reconstructing your life starts with one profound shift. It will feel like an earthquake inside your soul, reorienting you toward life in a completely different way. That's you, starting over.

Resetting.

FALSE START

Your mindset and daily habits are the hidden forces holding you back. Growing up, we are told a confusing blend of stories by family, friends, the media, and other authority figures. Over the previous four chapters, we've seen how this clumsy narrative no longer applies.

The symphony of half-truths from all these sources infect each of us from an early age. Most of the assumptions— more information is better; education means endless hours sitting obediently in a chair; receiving free stuff is great—are mismatched to the evolving world. That means the advice based on those assumptions is also suspect. Even though the advice is delivered by good people with good intentions, the overall effect is still negative.

Thanks to this kind of upbringing, most of us ended up believing in boundaries, not possibilities. Rules, not inspiration. Checking the box, not creating beauty and meaning. These are the beliefs that will betray us when we try to build a good life for ourselves in the digital world.

We have to shake off the mindset of scarcity and limitations. We must take a look—maybe the first honest look—at our lives as adults. Are we getting what we want? Do our actions sync with our goals? Are we confident in our ability to thrive? Are we even confident we can *survive* from one day to the next?

Of course, it's not your fault you aren't prepared for the digital world. You didn't create modern society any more than I did. But that doesn't excuse us from trying. Each of us bears the responsibility to do something about our unique situation. (That one blunt fact is not even remotely fair, but it is true.)

Accepting responsibility for what you can control—your mindset and daily behavior—is where we all start. There is so much good waiting for you, and it will flow from this moment of radical choice. You will be free to build a life that actually takes you in the right direction. You will be able to take powerful action and build support structures that drive you toward success.

But first you need to Reset.

My friend Justin is a fascinating guy. He has gone through a lot in his short life, coming out of the military to community college and on to the Ivy League. He then made the leap from finance to technology to entrepreneurship, and he is enjoying a challenging but rewarding career. He is a thoughtful guy with a great wife, close family, and a solid group of friends.

Of course, his life isn't perfect. I'm not trying to make you envious. We're going to be inspired by him! Justin is an example of someone who was able to take his life to the next level by Resetting. He shifted his perspective to one of personal responsibility and developed daily behaviors to support his goals.

Justin is from Illinois. He was a great football player in high school. Not NFL great, but definitely a local standout. One summer, he and his team went to a training camp. After finishing up the grueling program, Justin and one of his buddies—also a top prospect—were waiting to take a cab to the airport. Some random guy walked up to them and asked if he could split the fare. Being poor high school students, they agreed.

It turns out this guy was a recruiter for Princeton. A chance encounter turned into the potential for a big break!

The first thing the recruiter did was ask them about their GPAs. Princeton puts the student before the athlete. Justin had a 3.5 and his buddy had a 4.0. Even though Justin was just as good an athlete, his 3.5 GPA was not going to cut it. The recruiter zeroed in on Justin's friend, snagged his contact information, and eventually tried to entice him to Princeton with a scholarship.

Justin's friend ended up going to a different Ivy League university, but it was that first conversation with a top-tier recruiter that opened his eyes. He started thinking about other great schools, not just the public universities in Illinois. That cab ride had a huge impact on his life.

Meanwhile, Justin took a different path. He joined the Army for a couple of years and then went to a community college back home. From there, he pushed himself to find a path to a great university, and he eventually landed at Cornell. He went on to investment banking in New York after that, he moved to San Francisco with his now-wife, and finally broke into a dream job in a fast-growing technology company.* Fast-forward a few years, and he is the founder and CEO of his own startup!

Justin is on fire for his life, waking up every day with a sense of purpose and profound gratitude for the blessings he received. Looking back, though, life threw Justin a lot

---

* That doesn't make money through advertising!

of curveballs. He had to scramble, shift course, start over, and find new routes. It took him five years just to get to the same stage as his high school buddy.

Like many of us, Justin had to take several detours. He got back on track not once, but several times. In his case, the first detour was through the military. For others, the detour may be a dead-end job, the death of a family member, pursuing the wrong education program, a sudden illness, or living in a different country.

HITTING THE WALL

The lesson from that cab ride was that Justin missed an important opportunity because he wasn't prepared. The interaction with this recruiter totally blindsided him. And it was the first time he ran up against an insurmountable wall in life.

Justin is an easygoing guy. He can usually talk his way through situations. This was especially true when he was growing up. But the Princeton recruiter did not want to negotiate. He had no interest in excuses or a sob story. So he ignored Justin completely.

Justin's failure at that moment had nothing to do with his innate skills or abilities. On the contrary, he later proved he was Ivy League material. The problem wasn't his potential.

The problem was the gap. The gap between where he needed to be and where he was. And his mindset shifted completely when that gap became obvious to him. The situation was so obvious, how had he never seen it? Why hadn't he taken responsibility for his grades? He wasn't going to be transported magically to the school of his choice. Life doesn't work that way.

That moment is something he thinks about almost every day. It's become a key motivation for his journey, something he ponders when he finds himself losing focus or drive.

I can't predict the future, but I seriously doubt Justin will ever be caught unprepared again. It's way more likely that he will be ready when the next great opportunity comes along. And then the one after that. And the one after that.

Justin will do whatever needs to be done to create the right conditions for him and his family. They will thrive because he will make sure of it. It's up to him.

THE CHOICE OF A LIFETIME

This shift in mindset is the beginning of a Reset. We have to deeply feel the need to change our lives. The pain of living every day like today must become greater than the pain of working to change.

And there will be pain. We have to ignore the rest of the world that wants to excuse our behavior or let us wallow in self-pity. Instead, we look inside ourselves for strength. This is the fuel we burn as we overcome all the challenges that inevitably result when we try to live a meaningful life. Your Reset will be powered by a fierce determination to matter, to yourself at first, and then to others.

Of course, we won't all have such a singular event. But ask yourself, what actually *happened* to Justin that was so special? He rode in a car with two other guys. That is the most basic description of the event. I ride in cars all the time, and it doesn't give me the fuel to improve my life!

It was Justin who used that situation as fuel to power his Reset. He had to *choose* to infuse that experience with meaning, and to keep coming back to it for years afterward. There are dozens of other moments in his life that could have served the same purpose. There is no perfect moment to Reset.

Well, except right now. Right now is the best—the only—moment to get started. Reset now.

Here is the truth we all need to hear. We are the ones who give meaning to our short lives on Earth, not some other person or outside force. The events themselves can be more or less dramatic, but they happen quickly and then are in the past. What we call our lives are memories. They exist as a story we tell ourselves about where we came from.

It is our responsibility to circle back to these stories, look on them, and cherish them. We have to turn them over and over in our minds, like precious stones. That is a choice we must make or avoid at our own peril. Why? Because the story we tell ourselves about our past is the prologue of the story we tell ourselves about our future.

TURNING INWARD

The call to Reset is personal and intensely emotional. Initially, the focus must be internal. You should deeply *feel* the pain caused by the gap between your potential and your current situation. You have to embrace that feeling, however painful it is in the moment. As the Marine Corps slogan goes, "Pain is weakness leaving the body." Pain is a marker that shows us where we are hiding our deepest fears and dreams.

The call to Reset is the moment you say "Enough!" and expose all your built-up ugliness to the light of day. The things you have avoided your entire life. The things that scare you the most about yourself. The things of which you are ashamed. The things that cause you to procrastinate. The failures. The abuses. The sadness. The hurt.

Your Reset is the moment you stop looking at the world as a source of your problems. Life is not something that happens to you. Life is something you choose to embrace.

You must claim radical responsibility for all your failures as well as your successes. Every excuse you've held onto for so long must be revealed as a lie. All the weight lies on your shoulders. You are the one who led yourself to the point in life where you are now. No one else can be blamed. And no one else can do what you need to do now. This heartbreaking revelation is the beginning of something amazing, even if it doesn't feel like it.

You've just stopped playing checkers and started playing chess.

ALL IN

Resetting won't be simple, and it won't be easy. There are long-held values to be examined, myths to be discarded. Often, we aren't even aware of how much we take for granted in the world. We marinate in the attitudes and indulgences of our own society, so we can't see it objectively. There are so many expectations and norms. So much background noise that only confuses us.

You will have to reject some—possibly all—of the one-size-fits-all values. You will be surprised how often you are pursuing something for the wrong reasons. You may have accepted something as necessary when you don't actually want it.

Home ownership, does that make sense? Maybe, maybe not. Two weeks of vacation a year, does that make sense? Maybe, maybe not. Same thing for marriage. And kids. And your career.

Ask yourself: what will be the building blocks of my *real* life?

There is no such thing as a partial Reset. Resetting is a fundamental reexamination of your life. It's the radical step of taking full responsibility for the outcomes in every area of your life. And rather than being upset or annoyed, from now on, you will *expect* that your actions will be neither easy for you nor popular with everyone else. When you take charge, it's a reminder to everyone around you that this personal transformation is also an option for them.

Most of them will shy away from this profound choice. They will be confused or scared when they see you change and take on new behaviors. It won't make sense to many of them, because you will be making decisions based on a powerful but dangerous truth: you are in control...but only if you are willing to be.

I can close my eyes and think back to the days when my daily path was a downward spiral. My heart beats faster just dredging up those memories. Back then, life seemed to be collapsing. I was in complete disarray. Each day felt worse than the one before.

I was getting an "F" in life.

The feeling of dissatisfaction intensified after I decided to join the Marines, which we will talk about more in later chapters. This surprising reaction to an otherwise good decision was the first manifestation of my internal resistance to change. And it caught me completely off guard.

That's how it feels during the early stages of a Reset. It was actually easier to ignore my total lack of momentum before I had something to which I aspired! As soon as there was a destination I wanted to go toward, it became clear how far I had to go. And then all my old rationalization mechanisms kicked in.

"You're never going to make it. You aren't tough enough."

"They won't accept someone like you. You don't have what it takes."

"Just sit back down on the couch. Watch some TV. You can go for a run later."

We often struggle when we first accept the need to pursue meaningful goals. We are like children being forced to eat our vegetables. We kick. We scream. We stomp our feet and complain loudly that it isn't fair. And the funny thing is, we are complaining to ourselves!

PUSH PAST UGLY

There is also a tendency to beat up on ourselves when we begin a transformative journey. Our enthusiasm is high, but the results often lag behind our expectations. We look at our lives and start to assign blame for the lack of progress. We think to ourselves, "I'm doing something wrong. How did this happen? I'm so far behind where I thought I would be."

Of course, that's not fair or very helpful either. Remember, the first step of any journey can be ugly. The first version of *anything* is going to suck! Remember the first time you tried to drive a car or do long division?

I rest my case.

Don't get discouraged by the awkward beginning phase. We all start as ugly ducklings on our way to becoming swans. We get confused because the world only shows you swans. Advertising is all about the final product, perfectly packaged, and gleaming on the shelf. That's a trap. An excuse to never get started.

And how do you progress from the clumsy first version to something that makes you proud? Work at it. Actually, grind on it. There is no other way. It is the effort you put into the journey that makes the whole thing worth it.

Don't let yourself believe the convenient lies that saturate our culture. You're not going to trip and fall into a life of meaning and fulfillment. You won't accidentally make a lot of money or find the perfect spouse. Life isn't going to get any better unless you embrace the trials and tribulations. And that starts with aspiring to a better life.

This can be demotivating, especially in the short term. Those comfortable lies that let you continue your downward slide are gone. Now you are tackling each challenge head-on, even if you don't get it right the first time. But you keep going, putting one foot in front of the other.

Your Reset, however long it takes, is that fundamental shift in your mindset from accepting the easy task of mindless consumption all the way to vigorously pursuing the meaningful and hard. You must face a lot of hard truths to do that. Correct a lot of bad behavior. Make up for a lot of lost ground. Apologize to yourself and others for sacrificing your time at the altar of comfort and convenience.

While this may seem negative or self-critical, the early stages of a Reset are actually a huge gift. You now have a heightened sensitivity to the world and your place in it. It's a gift of perspective. Now can see what's *really* happening in the world around you. You will notice the people who limp through life with their phone surgically attached to their hand, choking continuously.

THE FEW

Only a small group of people will ever break apart from the crowd of distracted sheep that we have become. In the case of the digital world, it will be the ones who Reset that thrive in this arena of endless possibilities.

We get to choose the group to which we belong. Some of us have this epiphany at ten years old. For others, it may be in high school or college. Maybe it was at your first job. Or, it could happen when you move to a new town, lose a job, end a relationship, or begin a new one. Or, like many of us, you could still be waiting.

Let this be the moment when the truth finally sinks in deep enough to prompt serious action. You can pursue meaningful goals. You can adapt and thrive.

We can't look to the digital world for answers to the hard questions. All we find there is a bunch of illusions. Everyone is repeating the lie that an idealized life is actually possible. It's an echo chamber full of distracted people and distorted advertising.

The digital world tells us we should be living the perfect life right now. If we're not, then we suck. Because anything is possible. Everything we need to know is right there! Of course, that's a lie. As circus-clown-turned-entrepreneur—seriously—Derek Sivers puts it, "If information is what mattered, we would all be billionaires with perfect abs!"[1]

You should recognize this as the mantra of the digital world. Everything needs to be perfect. Everything needs to be perfect. Everything needs to be PERFECT!!!!!! It's the real-life version of "Everything Is Awesome" from *The LEGO Movie*.[2]

HARD TRUTH

You can't construct a fulfilling life out of humble brags and Photoshopped pictures posted to social media. Those things are meaningless—background noise. Remember that most of what you see in the digital world is designed to do only one thing: get your attention. You are the product, and you are worth a lot of money to those big advertising companies.

So don't look outward. Turn inward instead. That is where you find the strength to change, first your mindset and then your behavior. Like Justin after that cab ride with the Princeton recruiter, you can decide to build a new life from a particularly painful failure or missed opportunity. Like me, you will probably experience some discouraging moments before you break through. But man, is it worth it!

Resetting is the gateway to a fulfilling life. Now we need to learn who can show us what it takes to get there.

▣—▣—▣

What to remember about "Reset":

- Each of us has a different journey to taking responsibility for our life.
- We can be motivated by the gap between our potential and reality.
- Resetting will force us to discard traditional views that no longer apply.

Take five minutes to consider the following questions:

- Do you feel like you are close to operating at your full potential?
- Which fantasies do you cling to about your life?

- What are the forces, people, and constraints holding you back in life?
- How could you overcome these issues?
- What events in your life could motivate you to get started?

If you want to spend fourteen minutes learning more about Resetting, watch Ruth Chang's great TED Talk, "How to Make Hard Choices."[3]

If you want to spend two hours learning more about Resetting, watch *The Matrix,*[4] or watch the three-minute clip[5] that spells out your choice to Reset.

If you want to spend four hours learning more about the early struggles of Resetting, read Steven Pressfield's book, *The War of Art.*[6]

CHAPTER SIX

DIGITAL MESSIAHS

WHO CAN BE OUR GUIDE IN A RAPIDLY CHANGING WORLD?

"The future is already here—it's just
not very evenly distributed."

—WILLIAM GIBSON, CANADIAN AUTHOR

A small group of people already know how to thrive in the digital world. They seek out opportunities to create new things. They learn what works and what doesn't work through years of hard work, soul-searching, and feedback. And since they found out what works, that means we don't have to. We get to fast-forward our own progress by looking to them for inspiration.

I'm talking about a very unusual breed of entrepreneurs, consultants, and freelancers. Specifically, people in these categories who have built profitable, fulfilling businesses according to the rules of the digital world. They have cracked the code on the creative economy that we discussed in Chapter Two. I will refer to this ambiguous group collectively as "entrepreneurs" for the sake of clarity.

Entrepreneurs are important because they represent an extreme end of the spectrum. Building a new business from scratch is brutal. In fact, at least 92 percent of new companies will fail, and that figure is probably much closer to 99 percent![1] Clearly, the odds are stacked against the entrepreneur when starting a new company. He or she is shaping the world in ways no one else ever has.

Despite such an incredibly demanding environment, entrepreneurs somehow manage to thrive. The successful ones figure out a way to beat back distractions, find a valuable niche, build a great team, and sustain momentum long enough to achieve a nearly impossible dream. That ain't easy!

We need to pay close attention to the few who managed to pull it off. The mindset and behaviors of these successful entrepreneurs are a rich source of clues to help us think through our own lives.

To be clear, I'm not saying we all need to build businesses. You don't need to be an entrepreneur to benefit from the lessons they have to offer. The point is we can look to these extreme cases to extract the best strategies and tactics. These are the clues to what might work in our own lives.

What if you wanted to get in great shape? Would you want an average-looking personal trainer? Of course not. You would want someone who practices what they preach. A really fit trainer probably knows a lot more about what works in practice, not just the stuff that *sounds* good.

The same logic applies to the newest crop of entrepreneurs. The ones who are succeeding despite digital distractions. They can show us what is practically useful, which lets us leapfrog over a lot of potential mistakes. We avoid a lot of frustration and wasted time.

ENTREPRENEURS, ASSEMBLE

I run an entrepreneurial education program at Stanford called the Silicon Valley Innovation Academy, or SVIA.[2] The seven-week course runs each summer for visiting students, mostly international folks. They want to learn more about how they can tap into the Silicon Valley magic and build their own great companies. They are the definition of hungry: full of enthusiasm and limitless energy. Just being around them energizes me!

These entrepreneurs start the summer by assembling into small groups. Each group organizes around a specific vision for a new startup. We help them identify potential customers based on their idea. Then they try to talk to these potential customers about their product or service. This lets them know if their startup is actually addressing a real need out in the world.

The groups assemble at least once a week and update my team and me on their progress. This rhythm continues throughout the summer, so we get to see the rapid evolution of each startup. The teams go from vague statements about customers to being focused like a laser on specific problems their team can address.

Every entrepreneur will hear "No!" hundreds or thousands of times when starting a new company. Our SVIA startups are no exception. These kids—most of them nineteen or twenty years old—are constantly having doors slammed in their faces, being rejected via email, and getting the runaround on the phone. For seven weeks straight.

How long would you keep going in such a situation? A few days? A few weeks? Imagine the resiliency you would need to maintain your enthusiasm, not to mention the stress you and your team would be under.

How much would you need to believe in your dream?

IS IT WORTH IT?

In a recent SVIA, a young woman—let's call her Melissa—came to me during office hours about halfway through the program. We sat outside at Coupa Cafe in the Stanford Graduate School of Business on a beautiful summer day. Normally these sessions go through a predictable process: talk about what isn't working; talk about potential fixes to these problems; and talk about immediate next steps.

Melissa wasn't interested in any of that. She cut right to the core of the issue that was plaguing her. She plopped down in the chair to my left, stared bleakly at me, and asked, "Is this worth it?"

I could see tears starting to form in her eyes. She looked like she was going to crumple into her chair. And I had nothing but sympathy for her. I've walked the same path. I've shed the same tears. Melissa came into SVIA full of confidence with a clear vision of the future she wanted to build. But with three straight weeks of rejection by the people she thought she was helping, the cracks were starting to show.

Melissa cared so much about her idea. I had seen the passion on day one, when she fearlessly stood up in front of a packed auditorium to recruit other people to join her team. Back then, it had been so simple. "Here's the idea. Isn't it great? Don't you want to join my team, everyone?"

And now, not even a month later, the world seemed to be conspiring against her.

Now she was starting to understand just how hard entrepreneurship can be. She had lots of other options back home. No one would blame her for giving up now. But then her vision for the future would never come to pass. No one would ever have their lives transformed by her company. The world would remain unchanged. This was the realization with which she was struggling on that sunny morning at that small cafe tucked into a corner of the Stanford campus.

"Is it worth it?"

LOOKING AHEAD

Entrepreneurs can show us how to live with purpose. This rare breed of person takes on the responsibility of building that purpose for themselves, and eventually for their employees. Most of us simply *inherit* a purpose from others. *Building* purpose is a whole other level of passion and commitment.

Our job is to learn from this unusual class of people who have done amazing things. Why? Because they already picked up a lot of hard lessons along the way. We get to push past a lot of the nasty stuff and go straight to the behaviors that work.

What do entrepreneurs have to teach you? A lot, actually!

We are all stuck in the same digital world. We are all constantly tempted by the same distractions. What's important to understand is how much some of us are able to beat the odds *despite* those distractions.

Here's the simplest way to put it: entrepreneurs get a lot done. Most of us do not. What's the difference? Let's explore five behaviors that tend to separate entrepreneurs from other people: having a vision; using tools; bending the rules; continuous prioritization; and ruthless focus.

A Vision of What Could Be

Entrepreneurs distinguish themselves by emphasizing a natural tendency to be more mission-oriented. They are driven to do something big, a future they believe can be created. They see the way the world works right now, and they want to change it. Entrepreneurs tend to default to the inspiring goal, not the messy details. The business itself is not the point, which often surprises people. A business is just a mechanism for facilitating the change they want to see in the world. The vision for the future is what matters. And it is this vision that changes the way a person thinks and acts.

Everything Becomes a Tool

To make that dream a reality, entrepreneurs learn to manipulate the world around them. Everything gets relabeled. People, companies, money, and information are all lumped into the same category: tools. All these things we see as separate are instead tools to use in the pursuit of the entrepreneur's vision. If something does not help them accomplish their goal, then it doesn't matter. Functional value is all they care about.

Suggestions, Not Rules

Entrepreneurs bend the rules when it suits them. They break rules, too. They will do whatever it takes to change the world. Many of us accept the way things are because we have no reason to dig any deeper. But an entrepreneur is constantly asking why things are the way they are. And dismissive answers will not dissuade them from investigating and manipulating whenever possible. Nothing stands in their way. This resourcefulness is a critical trait for anyone trying to build a new company from scratch.

Avoiding Time Wasters

Distractions are even more of a hazard for an entrepreneur than for regular people. New companies involve a lot of moving parts. There are legal, financial, and operational issues popping up constantly. There's the recruiting of people to their team. Don't forget the constant challenges related to product development. And, of course, the never-ending requests from customers, investors, partners, and so on. It's easy for an entrepreneur to allow the situation to become overwhelming. A lot of entrepreneurs make that mistake when they start. Success will require them to identify and focus their time on accomplishing the things that really matter.

Focusing on Outcomes

Results are all that matter, not intentions or appearances. The contract was signed, or it wasn't. The money arrived into the bank account, or it didn't. There isn't much of a choice for anyone who is serious about building a business. Either figure out what will work or go get a job and stop pretending to be an entrepreneur. The worst outcome would be getting stuck in purgatory for years waiting for a break that never comes.

Clarity and confidence separate the foolish and the wise. The amateur and the professional. The failure and the success.

Making things complicated is easy. Simplifying is hard. At the core of every business are just two activities. Build a product or service that people are willing to pay for. And sell that product or service to lots of people.

Build and sell. Build and sell.

This is where distraction becomes so different for entrepreneurs compared to other people. Moments count in the early days of a business. Everything and everyone must be aligned for the company to survive. Of course, mistakes are inevitable when you are doing something completely new. Where there is no room for error, though, is time. Entrepreneurs don't have the luxury of wasted time. They need to be moving as quickly as possible toward building the right product and selling it to the right customers.

And that is why we can learn from them. Because they have learned how to be laser-focused despite all the distractions of the digital world.

LEARNING CURVE

I've worked directly with hundreds of entrepreneurs and trained thousands more through custom programs that I've built for companies, military organizations, nonprofits, and universities at my companies, BMNT and NeuBridges. I know that entrepreneurs are truly a remarkable group, capable of jaw-dropping productivity both individually and as the leader of a group.

When I first started working with entrepreneurs, I thought the "secret sauce" would have something to do with how they were being educated. Maybe it was the curriculum or the professors. The difference must be what they were learning, right?

Wrong. It turns out these pieces don't matter. There is no correlation between higher education and the eventual success of the entrepreneur.

Success is not about *learning* for an entrepreneur. Success is based on *doing*. Learning is part of the process—another tool you can use—but it is not the goal.

It turns out there are only three repeatable things I can do to help propel a committed entrepreneur forward: clarify their vision for the company; help them reshape their environment; and propel them to take action as early and often as possible. I also give feedback on pitch decks and make introductions, of course, but I've found these significantly less valuable. They don't lead to those outcomes that truly matter to a young business.

We will cover these briefly right now and then dive deeper into each one as it relates to our lives. In Part III—the next three chapters—we will unpack these concepts so you understand exactly why they are so critical for your Reset.

Let's start with a mission. The single most important service I can provide to an entrepreneur is to remind them why they are in the program in the first place. Their vision for the future will drive them forward. They need to be asked questions that force them to clarify their mission.

"What problem are you trying to solve?"

"How are you changing the world?"

"Why would people remember your company in fifty years?"

The clearer the answer, the greater the focus and energy. The more compelling the vision, the better they are able to overcome the inevitable fear and anxiety.

Entrepreneurs who are on a mission quickly realize how much progress is lost to distractions. It's death by a thousand tiny cuts. Choking—mindlessly consuming content—becomes physically painful to them. Every minute spent distracted is a minute they are not building their company. Every minute spent distracted means they are that much farther away from having an impact on the world. They are failing in their mission to build something meaningful. That is a powerful and emotional pull to a passionate entrepreneur.

Most people I work with do not start at this level, though many get there eventually. They begin by *aspiring* to be entrepreneurial, which is often the opposite of actually being an entrepreneur.

Aspiring entrepreneurs actually waste a lot of time. They act like entrepreneurs, doing things they read about or see in media or hear from their friends. They have lots of meetings over coffee, read articles about entrepreneurs, talk about their product that isn't yet built, and make fancy PowerPoint decks to ask investors for money.

Eventually, they learn that stuff is worthless, and they start doing the tough work of building a business. Or, they give up and get a job. Either way, the power of that clear vision helped them arrive at their destination much faster.

ACTIONS

Entrepreneurs choke just like the rest of us. But remember that you and I still get paid when we're choking if we have a job. Your pay doesn't get docked if you're on Instagram or YouTube.

But no one gets paid during the early days of a company. The whole team is sprinting, full steam ahead! The sheer velocity of startups is enough to scare away most people. You need a lot of risk tolerance to do well as an entrepreneur or part of an early team. Reid Hoffman, billionaire founder of LinkedIn, has a memorable way of describing the experience. "An entrepreneur is someone who jumps off a cliff and builds a plane on the way down." Many of us are not ready for something like that, even if we *think* we are.

Speed is a consequence of action. Specifically, entrepreneurs in the early stages of building a new business focus on two actions:

- Talking to potential customers
- Building early versions of the product

Both are absolutely critical for an entrepreneur. It's easy to get stuck in a room with your founding team, arguing about random features that won't be built for months. As crazy as it sounds, people fall in love with their ideas and can actually be afraid to talk to the very people who want to pay them money.

I acknowledge this strange tug-of-war whenever I'm coaching someone. That person needs to know it's normal for them to avoid getting in front of customers. Of course, that doesn't mean they don't have to. I provide the encouragement—sometimes even the introduction—that pushes them into the realm of taking action.

Here's a typical conversation to illustrate the point. Let's pretend an entrepreneur wants to build a company that sells widgets. It doesn't matter what the widget is. The point is that they are trying to sell them.

Entrepreneur: "So our widget is a huge improvement over the existing options. We are going to sell directly into this market and displace the competition."

Me: "That's interesting. How do you know your widget is a huge improvement?"

Entrepreneur: "It's obviously better. Look at how much faster our widget is compared to the current models."

Me: "And do customers care about widget speed?"

Entrepreneur: "Of course they do!"

Me: "How do you know that?"

Entrepreneur: "Because...everyone wants their widgets to be faster."

Me: "Maybe you should go talk to some people who actually buy these widgets."

Entrepreneur: "Um, okay. Where should I start?"

Me: "Well, I have two friends who run widget companies. You can start there. I would also suggest Googling 'widget companies' and see if you can find out who their main customers are. Then you can start reaching out to people through their contact page or LinkedIn. Try to interview at least ten of them in the next week, which will probably require that you email at least one hundred or so."

Entrepreneur: "Whew. Okay. That's a lot of work."

Me: "Yes, it is. Have fun! Tell me what you learned next week."

STRUCTURES

Structural control is the other valuable insight I can give to an entrepreneur. The right structure is crucial to someone building a company. We're talking about structure in the broadest sense. Everything from the people they meet with and the room where they work, all the way to the type of content they read. The structure of their daily lives.

The transition to successful entrepreneurship requires that a person take control over the structures that influence his or her behavior. People who are serious about their vision will consciously shape their world in ways that help them work toward that vision through productive action. They will want to spend more time on their company, while shrinking the time wasted on the random distractions that will pop up.

Everything, from getting rid of negative friends to removing apps on their phone, serves that core purpose of outcomes through intense, focused work.

Purposefully changing your environment also makes life easier and more enjoyable. Each of us has accumulated junk in our lives that takes up time and energy, crowding out the relationships and work that energizes us. Soon you will realize how much time we all waste bumping up against obstacles that are easily avoided.

That's it. The vision. The action. The environment. You just learned all you need to know! But just in case you feel compelled to dig deeper, we're going to explore these behaviors in more detail. We will walk through the process of clarifying your vision, reshaping your environment, and quickly taking action. And then we will go through the process of customizing and applying them to your daily life.

THE VERDICT

The final weeks of SVIA didn't get much better for Melissa after our meeting. She did push through the entire curriculum, learning a lot as she went. But it wasn't until the last week that she turned the corner.

Melissa's lightbulb moment was toward the end of the program when she realized many of the key partnerships the business needed were available through her university back home. She could actually build a program to accomplish her goal, but it didn't need to be a company. In fact, she could quickly create something that could be implemented in the next school year!

All the work Melissa put into her idea laid a strong foundation. She had a deep understanding of the problem she was trying to solve, but she couldn't make the business side work. Why? Because she didn't have to. Her mission could be accomplished without starting a new company. It was actually much easier than that. The mindset and habits she developed in SVIA would let her quickly develop and deploy her solution. Melissa got to build her dream, after all.

You will also have to ask yourself the question, "Is it worth it?" when you try to pursue a valuable mission. And like Melissa, the answer will take a form you could not have imagined at the beginning.

With entrepreneurs showing us the way, we can turn to the principles that will take your life to the next level. We're on to Part III, where we explore the three key elements of a Reset in the digital world.

▣—▣—▣

What to remember about "Digital Messiahs":

- Entrepreneurs are a source of inspiration for determining which behaviors are useful in the digital world.
- They benefit most from refining a vision, taking action, and shaping their environment.

Take three minutes to consider the following questions:

- Can I describe a vision for my life in detail?
- Have I considered how my environment affects my thoughts, feelings, and actions?
- What would my daily routine look like with fewer distractions?

If you want to spend ten minutes learning more about entrepreneurs and their lifestyles, read "Use These Daily Routines of 7 Famous Entrepreneurs to Create Your Own Routine"[3] by Siobhan Harmer.

If you want to spend four hours learning more about entrepreneurs and their lifestyles, read Ben Horowitz's book, *The Hard Thing About Hard Things*.[4]

PART III

THE FOUNDATION

CHAPTER SEVEN

MISSION MENTALITY

WHAT IS POWERFUL
ENOUGH TO INSPIRE ME TO
AVOID DISTRACTIONS?

"The purpose of life is a life of purpose."
—ROBERT BYRNE, AMERICAN AUTHOR

January 14, 2010, changed my life forever. I was in San
Francisco at the Marines Memorial Club & Hotel.[1] The
building is a historic landmark, dedicated shortly after
World War II. It's a focal point for military-related events
and communities in the Bay Area.

That day we were listening to a senior military commander

give a talk titled "The Way Ahead in Afghanistan." This particular general—Richard Mills—would be leaving the US soon to take command of the Marines in the volatile Helmand and Kandahar provinces. Sangin District, the area where I deployed later that year, was at the center of the conflict throughout 2010 and 2011.

But I knew none of this when General Mills walked up to the podium.

I sat at a round table, the remains of a meal scattered across my plate. With me at the table were seven other guys, all of whom had served in the Marine Corps or Navy. Surrounding us at a few dozen tables were hundreds of veterans from the major wars of recent American history: Iraq (both times), Afghanistan, Vietnam, Korea, and even World War II.

In early 2010, the United States was starting its "surge" in Afghanistan. Everyone knew that the next couple years would make a huge difference in the outcome of the war, and also the stability of the entire region.

As I sat listening to this general lay out his plan, I casually scanned the room. I was drawn to the faces of the older men. They were perched on the edge of their seats, eating up every word. As crazy as it sounds, these guys all wanted to deploy to Afghanistan! Most of them would have had to leave behind cushy jobs in banking, real estate, consulting, or technology.

These people didn't care about money, though. Not at that moment. Everything else about their lives receded into the background as they listened eagerly to details about the upcoming campaign that could decide the future of a nation, a people, and a whole region of the world.

All I remember thinking at the time was, "I don't want to be like that when I'm their age, wishing I had raised my hand to take on this challenge." Something had shifted inside as I listened to General Mills. Once again, I had that old, familiar feeling. I had a purpose. I was *on fire*.

Like the men around me, I had some fight left in me. But unlike them, I could actually do something about it.

And so I did, dropping out of Stanford to rejoin the Marines. I finished the quarter at Stanford in March and checked back into Camp Pendleton in Southern California by the first week of April. By the middle of August, I was saying goodbye to my family and heading over to Afghanistan.

Many of my civilian friends didn't understand. My behavior was borderline insane. Drop out of a great school to go to war? Why? They couldn't see the value of the mission, or how I fit into it. But that's okay. I didn't blame them. They weren't me and didn't have my experiences. I could clearly see how much I needed to walk down this path.

School wasn't cutting it. I couldn't sit in a classroom. Not when there was a chance I could make a real difference instead.

HUNGRY FOR PURPOSE

The Ancient Greeks used the word *telos*. The best translation is "end-purpose" or "end-goal." I love this concept. The *telos* of a thing. What is its purpose? Why does it exist? As we saw in the last chapter, this is a key element that entrepreneurs coax out of themselves, even if they need a little help sometimes.

Our *telos* unlocks enthusiasm and drives us by providing a true north. The *telos* becomes our mission. Our purpose. Our reason for taking every breath.

Most people do not think about the world like this. We get dragged away from the most important considerations by a constant barrage of pointless junk. We stare down at our feet as we shuffle through life.

The natural frictions of life—bills, traffic, paperwork— force us to spend our precious time worrying about the details. This dynamic existed before the digital world, but now it's on steroids!

We often forget why we are doing something in the first place. Whatever our original objective, we let the smaller, intermediate tasks get in the way. Missing the forest for the trees, as the saying goes. We rob ourselves of the ability to see how the dots connect. This is such widespread behavior that it even has an official clinical name: goal displacement.[2]

Our tendency to get distracted with details is precisely why we need missions! A mission lifts up your gaze, forcing you to look up so you can stare confidently at the horizon. The mission reminds us why we do what we do. This is a rare trait in a world where everyone seems content to plod along mindlessly.

A mission motivates us to the point where we will let nothing stand in the way of making it a reality. Doubts are unavoidable, but they can be overcome when we can see the clear connection between our current actions and our ultimate goal. Every obstacle is just a stepping stone on the path.

A mission reorganizes the way you think. A compelling mission reframes the resources around you. Everything becomes a tool to help you build your dream. Everything, even money, is evaluated based on how it can move you closer to the *telos*.

A mission also inspires the people around you. There is a glorious power and freedom to the feeling that we are doing what we are meant to do. And that is exactly what happens to a team when it collectively adopts a mission. People are freed to do their best work in the service of a compelling cause.

Marc Benioff, the billionaire founder of Salesforce, learned this the hard way. He struggled for years as an early executive at Oracle. The company wasn't able to plan effectively because the business environment changed so quickly. Without a plan, communication broke down.

Marc's response was developing the now-famous V2MOM tool. It starts by clarifying the vision of the company.[3] Everything else hinges on that vision. That goal. That mission.

PARADOX OF CHOICE

Unfortunately, compelling missions seem to be few and far between. If you're like me, you've been interested in lots of different ideas, people, jobs, companies, and places. There are so many options out there! How can anyone ever truly know what they want out of life? It's so hard to choose. I could never pick just one and stick with it for the rest of my life. That's completely unrealistic.

Don't fall into this trap. No one has complete confidence in a choice when making it. We can't set such a high bar before making a choice. None of us has unshakable confidence in our personal and professional goals.

That's true even for the folks who tell you they always knew they wanted to be a doctor, engineer, a social worker, or whatever. They don't always feel that way in the sense of complete certainty. But their *telos* is always stronger than the inevitable doubts.

Clearly knowing our mission means we have memorized the story we tell ourselves every day about why we get out of bed every morning. No matter how we feel, we still get up.

FOCUS, FOCUS, FOCUS

Focusing on a mission is a skill. A lucky few—such as the entrepreneurs in the last chapter—are born with enough of this mission mindset that it naturally modifies their behavior. They are totally obsessed with a particular opportunity and will take incredible risks to take one good shot at it!

Elon Musk is the extreme example of how a mission mentality can affect our behavior. The billionaire entrepreneur built Zip2 and PayPal, netting himself almost $200 million by 2002.[4] And did he put that money in the bank? No, he promptly plowed it into his next three companies: SpaceX, Tesla, and SolarCity.[5] And I mean, *all* of it. In 2008 he was completely out of cash and both companies almost went bankrupt.[6] That's how much some entrepreneurs believe in their missions.

The rest of us aren't like that, of course. And I'm not sure we should aspire to be. The point is that we can achieve many of the benefits of this kind of mindset.

We can train ourselves to identify and pursue compelling missions.

Finding a mission is easier said than done, though. Many people and organizations failed to build and maintain a mission mentality. Often, the *telos* fails to catch hold or quickly dies out. It's hard to define and then pursue a mission.

One of my professors at Stanford, Rob Reich, understands how difficult it is to choose in a world full of options.[7] On the last day of his classes, he offers the students a simple but provocative challenge: learn to close doors. Don't become obsessed with keeping your options open.

After years of watching students struggle, Professor

Reich now thinks the single most important lesson he can impart is that everyone needs to learn to commit. Avoiding choices is itself a choice. Seek out discomfort. Make the hard choices that will ultimately reward you.

Many of us have heard the saying—attributed to the ancient Greek philosopher Socrates—that the unexamined life is not worth living. Professor Reich turns this on its head, reminding students that the unlived life is not worth examining.

I WANT YOU

To find practical examples of how someone has become infused with a mission mentality, we can first turn to the United States military. Of course, the military has its flaws. I could write for hours about the problems of our armed forces.

That said, you do have to give credit where credit is due. The military is the only long-standing human institution that is built around missions. The martial culture requires missions. It *feeds* on them. Missions are the key ingredient for any military to be consistently successful not just on the battlefield, but also during the long periods of intense training between wars.

What does it mean to be mission-driven? How do you get

young men and women to suffer through months or years of hardship and danger for almost no pay? The answer lies in the way the organization creates meaning through common purpose.

START WITH WHY

Everything in the military is about an objective. There is always a light at the end of the tunnel. Some goal, some purpose. Some *Why?*

The military's emphasis on *Why?* is part of the explanation for its lasting ability to forge teams. That is the only way to bring a diverse group of human beings together with no shared heritage and get them to function as a cohesive unit. A compelling *Why?* changes the nature of any group. A bunch of individuals from every race, education level, and socioeconomic status become members of a group that would die for each other.

The military designs its training and organizational structure around the need for team-based development. At twenty, I was in charge of a fire team, which is four guys. By age twenty-two, I was in charge of a squad with a dozen guys. They were all about my age, maybe a year or two younger. It's crazy to think about that now. I had to deal with every aspect of their lives: physical, mental, moral, financial...you name it.

The military excels at combining high levels of responsibility with an overarching sense of mission. I felt connected to something that was both valuable and much larger than me. So did everyone else. The result? Rapid personal and collective development. Lots of mistakes, and lots of learning.

That kind of environment forces you to develop very fast. Much faster than you ever would have believed possible.

Whether or not you agree with the American military and its worldwide role, you should be able to admire the results. And like the latest generation of entrepreneurs, we can learn from them. There are some elements of the military's proven methodology from which we can draw. We can use this mission mentality to avoid distractions, push ourselves to new heights, accomplish amazing things, and become more fulfilled.

There is nothing in this world that feels like being part of something greater than yourself. Something that is a force for good in the world. Something that you know has an impact on other people. It's a beautiful feeling.

Why? is only half the equation, though. Next, we turn to the *Who?* This is the most overlooked element of a lasting mission mentality.

We respond particularly well to a mission when it places someone at the center. That means you are able to measure success by the impact you have on other people. Solving problems is important. But we often forget that behind every problem is the person who has it.

Improvised explosive devices—IEDs—are a huge problem in many areas of the world. Hundreds of people die each year, and thousands more are maimed. Men, women, and children. A select few people in the US military are trained exclusively to deal with the threat of IEDs. They are called Explosive Ordnance Disposal technicians, or EOD techs. You may have seen the movie, *The Hurt Locker*, where the main character was an EOD technician.

Or at least he was a fictionalized, Hollywood version of an EOD technician.

There is an organization tasked with helping all the EOD technicians.[8] These men and women work all year round, finding life-saving technologies and techniques. That is their mission: to protect EOD technicians. And they reinforce that mission in a powerful way. Every time an EOD tech is killed, they put up a memorial plaque along the main hallway of their headquarters. This reminds everyone why they are there, and the human cost of their failure.

The organization takes their mission and turns it into a compelling phrase that they constantly repeat to each other: keep them off the wall. In other words, our job is to keep these people alive.

That's the essence of a mission mentality. This group of people working out in Maryland, far away from the dangers of Iraq or Afghanistan, found a simple and powerful way to connect their daily work to a powerful, emotional *telos*.

SHOW ME THE PEOPLE

You can take advantage of the same dynamic as those researchers and scientists. You can pursue your goals with growing determination after seeing the impact you can have on others. That's the *Who?* of your mission, which combines with your *Why!* to take you to new heights!

Without changing anything else about your life, you can become more fulfilled almost instantly. How? By simply taking the time to notice the impact you have on your family, friends, coworkers, and customers. You'll be amazed how much you matter to other people.

An offhand comment you made was exactly what someone else needed to hear. A now-forgotten action made all the difference to a person in need of a helping hand. You don't realize how many times a day you are blessing others!

My wife experienced this at her last job. She used to work for Apple's enterprise software business. They help people build custom business applications. But what does that mean in practice?

This bland description took on a whole new meaning at a recent Developers Conference they held in Las Vegas.

My wife met a bunch of her customers and partners face to face. She heard story after story about how people are using this product to keep their businesses alive in a competitive global economy. A single mother even told her how she used FileMaker to make enough money to put her children through college.

Can you imagine how differently she felt about her company's impact after the conference? She clearly saw both the *Why?* and the *Who?* of her job. She went from thinking about the abstract value of building custom applications for businesses to picturing children in their cap and gown at a high school graduation. A proud mother taking pictures in the background.

Her company helped make that moment possible. That's purpose. That's *Why*.

DOLLAR SIGNS

Cultivating a mission mentality will require that you reframe the major activities in your life. You must be able to see—and eventually feel—the benefits of focusing on purpose and impact. This will happen primarily in one powerful way: money loses its place as the most important thing in your life.

This is a key piece of the entrepreneur's toolkit. Hopefully, we can exploit it for our own benefit, too.

An entrepreneur learns quickly that they can't be obsessed with money, especially when he or she is starting out. It's incredibly hard to sell stuff to people when you are a no-name company that has only existed for a month or two. You are an obviously risky choice. Why would someone pick you over something they've used for years?

Because your solution is exactly what they need. Successful entrepreneurs quickly learn to become experts in their customers' problems. Then they work tirelessly to solve them. Sometimes for free.

Entrepreneurs become obsessed with providing value to people, not with making money.

You and I don't naturally think like that. We like to picture the money, not the people who will pay us. This constantly frustrates me when I'm talking to the Stanford entrepreneurs[9] I teach.

In one mindset—let's make money!—these aspiring entrepreneurs have a hard time coming up with ideas, but in the other mindset—let's help people!—they are full of ideas. One is a wasteland, and the other is a blooming garden.

We were so obviously built to focus on others. Money corrupts our mindset and our actions.

We've all said something like, "I want to be a millionaire!" Statements like this are a strange blend of sad and funny. What people mean when they say stuff like that is, "I want to spend a million dollars." And spending money is the opposite of how you become rich!

The mission mentality takes us in a radically different direction than obsessing over money. We need to stop thinking about becoming rich and instead ask questions that require the courage of an idealist:

- "What kind of an impact do I want to have on the world?"
- "What is a problem to which I can devote my life?"
- "How do I want to be remembered?"

Those kinds of deep questions feed your soul. They also

help you probe deeply, which begins the slow process of excavating your true self. Asking these hard questions is the first step to finding something exciting. Something that is worthy to be called your next mission. Your next *telos*.

BILLIONS

Peter Diamandis, the chairman of XPrize and the cofounder of Singularity University, says it best. "You want to make a billion dollars? Help a billion people."[10]

When we learn to think and talk with a mission mentality, we inspire ourselves and others. Imagine talking with a friend about changing her career. The natural tendency is to talk about the practical aspects. Which job pays better? What sort of boss would you have at the new job? Would you need to go back to school?

These details are all relevant to some degree, but they miss the most important point. Your friend is trying to figure out what sort of mark she will leave on other people in this world. And yet we fear asking her that question. It is too profound. It seems too naive.

Instead, we focus on the surface issues, putting on a show of taking the conversation seriously.

My grandfather learned to fly during World War II. Like

a lot of wartime pilots, he joined the ranks of American Airlines to continue his career as a pilot. The early 50s were a tough time for the emerging airline industry, though. My grandfather was laid off. He had to take his wife, son, and daughter—my mom—to live in a converted garage at his parents' house in the Bay Area.

As my grandfather struggled to figure out what to do, his dad knew exactly what question to ask. And it wasn't about money, or job stability, or other details. My great-grandfather turned to my grandfather and asked him a question that erased all his doubts.

"Do you like to fly, son?"

COALITION OF THE WILLING

Thinking in terms of a mission challenges us. We are forced to address the serious question of our life, and the impact we want to have. This makes us uncomfortable. Fortunately, there is a built-in support mechanism. Family, friends, and peers. A mission that inspires you will also inspire others. That commonality is part of the beauty of being human.

As we'll see in later chapters, teams naturally form around good missions. All kinds of folks will emerge from the random corners of your life to help in unexpected and profound ways. A mission fuels collaboration. Money, by contrast, often stokes unhealthy and stressful competition.

Imagine each mission as a star. People are like the planets that end up in orbit of the star. The more compelling the mission, the greater the gravitational pull. The greater the gravitational pull, the more people end up in orbit.

Have you heard the story of Edward Shackleton? He led a group of men on an epic attempt to make it all the way across Antarctica. How did he receive over 5,000 applications from people to join his expedition? According to popular legend, by posting this advertisement: "Men wanted for hazardous journey. Low wages, bitter cold, long hours of complete darkness. Safe return doubtful. Honor and recognition in event of success."[11]

It's all about the mission.

These people who answer your call to a new mission will push you to great heights. They will build a new environment around you. It will stimulate and challenge everyone in it, especially you.

That intense, mission-driven, collaborative dynamic is fuel. Burning it will give you the energy to do seemingly impossible things! You will slingshot past your individual capabilities. You will build up yourself and others. And you will get better over time.

A small group of inspired people are the only people who manage to change the world, to paraphrase Margaret Mead.[12] A mission-driven team is the only environment where you're consistently expected to do incredible things. Things that appear to be well outside your abilities.

PLAY THE LONG GAME

You will need a mission if you want to avoid distraction and be fulfilled each day. In fact, you will need a series of missions, each one more demanding than the last. That's why it's called the mission mentality. It's a way of orienting yourself toward the world, not just one specific goal.

You must seek out missions, finding ways to weave your passions and skills into projects that help other people in meaningful ways. This mission mentality is the only way to pursue positive impact without sacrificing your ability to enjoy each day. It's the only way to relish each set of challenges and opportunities as they come. Why? Because a mission lets you get excited about sacrificing the efficient and easy for the meaningful and hard.

You can be enthusiastic and grateful for the chance to give it your all. A worthy mission demands nothing less!

I treat each mission like it was my purpose in life. I think carefully about the *Why?* and the *Who?* of each mission, revisiting these questions and my answers regularly.

As an example, consider Stanford's Silicon Valley Innovation Academy that I described earlier. My mission is to build the best entrepreneurial education program in the world. We don't want entrepreneurs building the next gaming app for a mobile phone. No Angry Birds version 7.1. We want them tackling tough problems.

You won't find the phrase, "The best entrepreneurial education program in the world" on a legal contract or the program's website. It's not on the back of any T-shirt. But that phrase is what I say to anyone who asks me about SVIA. It's what I say over and over to myself, the other people on my team, and the entrepreneurs. It's my reality. My mission.

My team challenges each other to do the best we can, every day during the summer. The entrepreneurs deserve nothing less. If we do our job, then they can build great companies that help create a prosperous future for the world.

And I don't have to deploy to a warzone to accomplish this mission. That's always a plus.

□—□—□

What to remember about "Mission Mentality":

- Focus on the question *Why?* to dig into your motivation for acting.
- Focus on the question Who? to explore the human impact of your actions.
- A compelling mission will naturally help you avoid getting distracted.
- A compelling mission draws in a team of willing supporters.

Take four minutes to consider the following questions:

- Do I have a good answer to Why? and Who? for my daily activities?
- What causes and organizations do I volunteer with or donate to?
- How do these causes and organizations draw me in?
- How would I feel if I could double or triple the impact I have in these fields?

If you want to spend ten minutes learning more about how we can create opportunities, watch Kare Anderson's TED Talk, "Be an Opportunity Maker."[13]

If you want to spend fourteen minutes learning more about creating emotional connections to work, watch Leonard Ha's TEDx Talk, "Who's on Your Poster?"

If you want to spend nineteen minutes learning more about how people are attracted to missions, watch Daniel Pink's TED Talk, "The Puzzle of Motivation."[14]

CHAPTER EIGHT

BIAS TOWARD ACTION

WHY AREN'T MY DREAMS COMING TRUE?

"Action is the foundational key to all successes."

—PABLO PICASSO, SPANISH ARTIST

How well did your sexual education class prepare you for having sex?

The answer is obvious, or at least I hope it is. There is only so much you can learn about sex in a classroom. And it's really not much beyond the basics of safety and hygiene.

However useful that instruction might be, the experience

of having sex is vastly different from sitting in a classroom learning about it.

In sex, as in most areas of modern life, we quickly bump up against the limits of traditional learning methods. Experience through action is the ultimate teacher. You need to develop some scar tissue.

The world wasn't always like this. Preparation before action used to be a lot more important. There were huge consequences to poor preparation if you were a hunter, farmer, warrior, traditional artisan, or factory worker. Humans had to be a lot more careful in those environments. One wrong decision or missed step in a process, and you could be left without food, killed by an enemy, or crushed by machinery.

Excessive planning and preparation makes a lot of sense with life-threatening consequences.

The digital world has completely flipped this dynamic. Now preparation can quickly become counterproductive. What used to be wisdom is now foolishness in many instances. But it's hard to let go of something that worked for so long. Our upbringing instilled us with a deep respect for preparation.

Excessive preparation worked in a world with scarce resources and long feedback cycles. A bias toward action doesn't make sense in such an environment because the incentives are so different than what you and I experience each day.

The obvious example of this older world is agriculture. You plant some crops and then wait months for the results.

The same principle is at work with large bureaucracies, where programs take months or even years to get off the ground.

These environments require a lot of effort to do anything because resources are limited, mistakes are costly, and time is measured in years. If you do manage to try something, the results come slowly. You better hope you didn't screw it up the first time!

These conditions—scarcity, high costs, slow feedback— don't exist in the digital world. We have our necessities covered and can get feedback on things almost instantly. We can take advantage of these incredible benefits to try all kinds of stuff, while learning and building confidence as we go. We need to ditch the plans.

Legendary boxing trainer Cus D'Amato famously said,

"Everybody has a plan until they get punched in the mouth." And you know what? We should all expect to get punched in the mouth once or twice when we try to do anything new. So just get out there and do it. Don't hide behind a plan.

THE CREATIVE PATH

Continuous and rapid learning through action is the only way to thrive in the digital world. Creative work through experimentation is one of the few areas left where people can obviously outperform computers. Our unpredictable imaginations cannot easily be replicated by advances in computing power, information storage, and powerful algorithms.

Human beings are the best animal in the world when it comes to creative behavior, and in the universe, so far as we know. That's why experimentation needs to be one of our guiding principles in the creative economy. The fastest way to get anything done is to start. Dip your toe in the water. Try a little bit. Do something. Anything!

The information we need to get started is always available in the digital world. We can quickly scout out what we need to know.

But that's not enough. What matters in a world of information abundance is not *accessing* the information but *using* it in some productive, creative, useful way.

Merely possessing the information means nothing. We need to act. Taking action is what changes things, from fixing the tiniest problem to averting a potential apocalypse. When you take action, the world is forced to adapt itself to you and your mission. That is the essence of creative work.

It is literally world-changing.

JUST DO IT

Action builds a different, more robust kind of confidence. When we take action, we develop the unique knowledge and experience that is critical for an impactful and fulfilling life. There is a depth of learning that cannot be replicated by someone who hasn't wrestled with the idea in an active way.

Most of us understand the need to act in an abstract sense. There is a deep, intuitive need we all share to grapple with the world around us. We want to shape things around us, to improve them. It's an innocent, naive, beautiful urge.

Unfortunately, we start doing the exact opposite as we progress through years of schooling. We learn passivity in the classroom, and we fall back on that behavior with our technologies. We stare at our screens, choking on wave after wave of digital garbage. The time for action came and went, and we just sat there.

We used to *do* a lot of stuff, especially as kids. We started with some wild notion somewhere in our brains. Then what did we do? We tested out that crazy idea.

We poked the electrical outlet with a fork. We drew on the wall with a crayon. We organized a group of friends to play a game. We messed with the world around us without worrying about the consequences.

As a parent, this drives me crazy. But I also recognize how much my kids learn. And how much fun they have while they're learning!

PROS AND CONS

The results from our impulsive actions are always some strange blend of good and bad. And that's what we should expect. You never get things right the first time. Or the second. Or even the tenth! But you keep pushing on, learning and improving as you go.

This sort of low-risk testing helps us analyze our efforts in an immensely practical way. Pursue your goals in the world, not inside your head! Early on, your goal should be to figure out whether or not something is worth your time. Were your assumptions true, or did it turn out that the situation was actually quite different? Quick feedback equips you with this kind of critical information.

Rapid growth is the key benefit of a bias toward action. Feedback from your actions leads to robust—and often unexpected—learning that you can then apply to other parts of your life. That's the difference between theory and practice. The mistakes you make in action are ones you will never make again. And you will never lose the confidence you build in action.

TURN THE CRANK

A bias toward action leads you naturally to iteration. That means doing something over and over again in rapid succession with improvements each time.

The military knows all about the value of learning through action. The After Action Review (AAR) is an activity at the end of every mission. Reviewing mistakes systematically is the fastest way to develop people individually and collectively.

This practice has been adopted formally since Vietnam, when it was needed to reform a huge draft military into an elite professional force. The results speak for themselves. Our military stands head and shoulders above anyone else.

Silicon Valley has also adopted a similar practice, although from a very different perspective. The "Godfather of Silicon Valley," Steve Blank, first wrote about this in his 2003 book, *Four Steps to an Epiphany*.[1] That was followed by Eric Ries's bestseller, *The Lean Startup*, published in 2011.[2] That's how new these concepts are. We're barely five years past the first popular book that summarized the best practices of Silicon Valley entrepreneurs.

In the business world, iteration is coupled with a Minimum Viable Product, or MVP. The starting point of this process is the MVP. It's the cheapest, simplest version of your core idea. Using the MVP approach means you build a new product or service in its most basic form. Then you test it over and over, modifying it based on what you learn. That is what it means to iterate.

An MVP is a guess about what a business should do. If you want to build some fancy service, for instance, there may be an email you can send out to a dozen people where they'll link to a website that asks people to pay for a basic version of that service. You don't have to build anything substantial yet, you just need to create a page and send it to a few friends who are similar to your imaginary customers.

Simple, easy, and fast. Very little cost to you, with the potential for massive rewards based on the quick learnings that can be applied to the business.

It's not just about entrepreneurship, either. The new practice of Design Thinking, popularized through the famous Palo Alto innovation consultancy called IDEO, also emphasizes the importance of a bias toward action. IDEO CEO Tim Brown's major book, *Change by Design*, gets into all the details of how they "fail early to succeed sooner."[3]

The surprising commonality between the military and Silicon Valley is the focus on what works. There is no fancy theoretical foundation here. It's all about results and the action driving those results. This approach works in an unusual variety of high-stress, high-stakes environments.

Building businesses and fighting wars. Who knew there was so much overlap?

BETRAYAL

Unfortunately for us, we have been trained to do the opposite of what's preached by these successful organizations. We saw in Chapter Two that our schooling made us passive, not active. We train to the test, regurgitating information all at once but then never returning to it again. In the same way, Chapter Three exposed the problem with our obsessive reliance on social media. We are stuck in an emotional storm, blown back and forth by both jealousy and fear.

Think about the things you want in your life. Maybe you need to start a business or move ahead in your career. Maybe you want to communicate better or improve a relationship. Or maybe you just need to get more done or contribute more to your company, family, or community. All those goals require the same thing.

Action.

What happens? The digital world gets in our way. Digital marketers exploit our natural desire for more information. They know there is always one more thing we can read, always one more post or article that is relevant enough to justify our attention.

The problem is that we quickly hit the limit of passive comprehension. Consuming can only take you so far. Of course, it's good to know some key details when you're starting something new, to have some idea of the lay of the land. But planning quickly becomes the enemy of action. Planning is the ultimate excuse for why we haven't started yet. We can still feel like we're doing something when really, we know deep down that we're stalling. Choking.

Change isn't easy. I behaved in counterproductive ways for years, banging my head against the wall.

I did my best to engage in activities that seemed to be useful. I would write out a plan with dates and activities, or I would create a spreadsheet that catalogued everything I was thinking about. I would write out a list of pros and cons for something. Or—my personal favorite planning tool—a checklist!

Finally, I realized the problem. I wasn't actually productive, but I *felt* like I was. I was trying to build up my confidence to some arbitrary level that would propel me to take action. When really all I needed to do was get started.

The digital world triggers some of the same *feelings* as taking action. Even with my military experience, I still reverted to passivity when my environment changed. The pull was so strong toward the screen. Plus, it was easy to convince myself I was being productive. Because I *felt* like it!

Research shows that when we form a goal—whether it's a project, some homework, or a simple task—if all you do is talk to other people about it, then you are actually *less* likely to follow through.[4] Why? Because you're getting some of the reward without actually having to do anything. It gives you the feeling you've accomplished your plan already.

Our tricky little brain is always trying to find a shortcut!

Realizing that problem was a key stage of my journey; at that point, I started grappling with the consequences of my behavior. I funneled energy away from pointless busy work, directing it toward productive channels instead. I focused on taking practical steps and learning based on the feedback, both good and bad.

I distilled each of my big ideas into a single, practical step I could accomplish in one day. I asked myself to imagine the worst outcome of that action, then the best outcome. If I could stomach the worst outcome and saw the value of the best outcome, I set a calendar reminder for the next day with a short description of that one big step.

And then, when that day came, I made sure to do it first thing in the morning. Then I paid attention to the feedback I received from that one big action. And then I went through the whole process again, this time starting with an improved idea based on what happened with that first action. Then I did it again. And again.

As I began taking action again, I encountered a very different feeling than choking or false productivity. I had earned the right to feel satisfied, versus tricking myself into that feeling of vague satisfaction from the standard *scroll*, *tap*, and *swipe* of the digital world.

Taking action lets you develop a sense of confidence you'll never get from planning, however beautiful or intricate the result.

SIZE MATTERS

Taking action consistently is difficult, particularly in the early stages. If you haven't already, you will soon discover it's actually tiny, inconsequential details that often derail your plan. These passive barriers are a huge problem when we try to make any positive changes in our lives, from saving money to improving diet.[5]

You must expect this hidden resistance and remove it as soon as possible.

Say you want to get more exercise. The practical action you choose is taking your dog for a walk every morning. And when it's time to leave the house, you may have a hard time finding the leash. Or the dog won't come when it's called. At that moment, it is so easy to throw up your hands and say, "I tried."

What if you are looking for a new job? You decide to look

at opportunities on LinkedIn, and quickly discover a few that could suit you. Then you realize you will need to send them your resume, but the only one you can find is over fifteen months out-of-date. Updating it will take at least an hour, possibly more if you get into a perfectionist trap. Again, you could just give up and say, "I tried."

These small frustrations are inevitable when you take action. Plan for them to emerge. The world will not just roll over when you decide to start taking charge. Don't let these small points of friction stop you. You will be surprised how much you can tolerate after you have adopted the mission mentality. The *Why?* and *Who?* will power you through the harsh realities of life.

Take action and have faith in that action. Develop your bias toward action. And you're about to find out just how powerful that can be when you have a structure to support it.

□—□—□

What to remember about "Bias Toward Action":

- Planning makes sense in a world of scarce resources with lengthy feedback.
- Action makes sense in a world of abundance with immediate feedback.

- A bias toward action is both a mindset and habit that can be cultivated.
- The world's best military and the world's best entrepreneurs use action as a way to quickly learn, improve, and succeed.

Take five minutes to consider the following questions:

- What would life be like if I accomplished one of my long-standing goals?
- What is a simple step I can take today toward that goal?
- What is the worst thing that can happen if I take this small action?
- What is the best possible outcome from that small action?
- How will I overcome the resistance that emerges?

If you want to spend five minutes learning more about the importance of taking action, read *Small Steps Will Take You to Big Goals*[6] by F. Diane Barth.

If you want to spend five minutes learning more about procrastination, read "The Science of Procrastination"[7] on The Brain Bank blog.

If you want to spend eight minutes learning more about the flaws of planning, read "Talent, Genius, and the Fog of Intention"[8] by Venkatesh Rao.

CHAPTER NINE

STRUCTURING SUCCESS

WHAT SEPARATES THE SUCCESSFUL FROM EVERYONE ELSE?

"The secret of your future is hidden in your daily routine."
—MIKE MURDOCK, AMERICAN SINGER AND SONGWRITER

A friend of mine, Jon, runs a program that promotes entrepreneurship in cities around the world for an international nonprofit organization. Jon meets a lot of amazing people. They are accomplished, wealthy, and respected. In a word, successful.

Jon spends a lot of time with these people. He works

closely with them, building communities to foster entrepreneurship as a way to develop the local economy. Jon gets to know each person intimately, and he recently shared a simple but profound insight with me. It had to do with success.

I've struggled for years to identify the thread that runs through the lives of successful folks. Each time I see a pattern, I get excited and start researching. Then everything falls apart as I dig into the research and data. I finally end up conceding I was wrong.

Jon was the one who finally connected the dots.

The secret is obvious and mind-blowing at the same time. All the successful people in the world are basically normal. In fact, they are *deceptively* normal.

The phrase Jon uses is "the deceptive banality of greatness." That's a fancy way of saying they are pretty much like you and me. And that is precisely what is so mindblowing!

Greatness does not manifest in crazy, over-the-top ways. Great people are mostly normal, with one major exception. They are abnormally effective when they take action. They are able to get a lot done, both directly and indirectly. Day after day after day.

Jon will tell you that these people are successful for reasons you and I probably haven't considered. Success—however we choose to define it—requires the careful cultivation of daily habits. It's not the glorious life we conjure up when we hear the word. Success could never live up to the expectations we heap on it. It's not about private jets, fancy clothes, or large estates.

STUDY OF SUCCESS

Let's consider the journey to "success" with the timeline of a person who earns that label. We'll call her Jessica.

Jessica works hard on things that really matter to her. Problems she wants to solve. She can easily see herself working on this problem the rest of her life.

Jessica pays attention to which activities lead to the desired outcome, and which ones waste her time. She invests more of her energy every day into those activities that matter. Her skills slowly expand and deepen.

Propelled by enthusiasm and hard work, Jessica reaches a level of mastery that is uncommon among her peers. She starts to stand out in terms of her ability to be useful to others in her chosen field.

Other people start to pay attention to Jessica now that her

daily efforts are yielding impressive results. They label her "successful" and tell others to "keep an eye" on her. She is "the real deal," "a rising star," and "a natural leader."

The legend starts to grow.

Meanwhile, Jessica keeps doing her thing, getting better and better at a relatively narrow set of activities. Oddly enough, it gets easier for her to have an impact in other fields as she cultivates her expertise. More people listen to her opinions. Resources flow more easily toward the things she decides to do.

Notice that Jessica's behavior isn't changing throughout this whole process. Her days look pretty much the same as they did a few years before. Same core activities, same slight corrections, and same steady improvements. Day in, day out. She maintains the same approach that got her the results in the first place.

The only change is the label we now attach to her. Now we pronounce her "successful."

LONG SHOT

This type of steady and relentless growth is what my friend Jon sees when he travels around the world to work with leaders. Successful people are actually normal people who are abnormally effective. The label of success is based on their ability to maintain these habits for years. The habits of getting things done. Things you will remember months or even years later. The important things. The things that can give birth to a legacy.

Successful people will never stop because these behaviors are so deeply ingrained. It's habitual. They have structured their lives to accomplish specific, meaningful goals. They focus on the things that matter to them. And then they didn't waver for a long time, even when they had temporary setbacks or unexpected problems.

This insight—success is habitualizing the daily work that matters to you—is easy to read (and to write) but incredibly hard to put into practice. Successful people are unusual in their patience, not their behavior. It takes a long time to build personal momentum and confidence. Like, a long time.

We should be thinking in terms of decades, not weeks.

EASY LIES

We want to believe that achieving success is not that simple—or that hard. It can't come from diligent effort applied over time. Instead, success must be about luck, like winning the lottery. Some of us can even point to a few overnight successes—friends who struck it rich through incredible circumstances—and use that to justify our own laziness or lack of progress.

Another ridiculous idea about success is that it's tied to happiness. Successful people are always happy, right? Success must be an incredible experience, an unending high. We imagine ourselves looking like the happy, smiling people we see in the endless advertisements that parade across our screens.

Because money solves everything, right?

These distorted images of success are part of the problem. We build this ridiculous wall between a successful life and where we are right now. We alienate ourselves from success by imagining it to be something complex and magical. We can't conceive of it as simple and kind of boring, honestly.

We want to believe in an easy answer. Money must be the difference between where we are now and where we want to be. That's because we're looking for answers on the outside, not from within.

CHANGE THE GAME

To become successful, you have to change yourself. But

not in some pop psychology way. You don't need to go to therapy. If you get nothing else from this book, pay attention to the next three sentences. They will change your life.

- Rebuild your mindset around compelling missions that help others.
- Take actions every day to accomplish your missions.
- Use a structure and support group to maximize the impact of those actions over time.

UNEXPECTED GIFT

I first learned the importance of structure as it related to supporting physical—not personal or professional—health. I am one of the 3 percent of formerly obese people who managed to keep off the weight for more than three years.[1] As of this writing, I have maintained a healthy weight—around 200 pounds on a six-foot-four body—for eighteen years.

The first time I tried to enlist in the Marine Corps, though, the recruiter laughed me out of his office because I weighed 300 pounds!

Although I was very upset at the time, I don't really blame the guy anymore. I was at least seventy-five pounds over the weight limit. Legally, he wasn't allowed to sign me up for boot camp. It wasn't the recruiter's fault. He was just playing the odds. Why waste time on a kid who has to lose that kind of weight when there are lots of qualified guys ready to sign up?

That was a low point. I had already told my family and friends I would become a Marine. With my plan starting to crumble, I had to make a big change, and it had to work!

My response was to focus on a new mission. Seventy-five pounds stood between me and the Marines, and I was determined to lose the weight. So, I started my own "pre-boot camp," and in the process, I stumbled onto the value of a demanding structure. I changed my life completely. It was the cleanest break from the past I could manage without isolating myself completely from my family.

I rented an apartment with two friends. The night we moved in—September 1, 2000—I went for the first jog of my life. Then I went out again the second day. And again the third day, fourth day, and so on. That nightly run became the foundation of a new workout regimen.

I added weight lifting once a week, then twice a week, then every other day. I started playing pickup basketball two nights a week. I cut back on food, especially at night. Eventually, I stopped eating desserts altogether. I also stopped smoking weed.

My mission of losing seventy-five pounds propelled me through eight months of intense training. I did not miss a single day of training. And it worked. My weight was down to 205 by the time I shipped off to boot camp in May of 2001. Then when I graduated boot camp in August, I only weighed 185. That's a total of 115 pounds lost!

LEVEL UP

I thought I already had a handle on things by the time I went to boot camp. But man, was I wrong. The Marine Corps took my concept of daily structure to a whole new level. What started as a way for me to lose weight grew into a completely different way of thinking about life.

Losing weight can be tough, but it's nothing compared to the mission of molding a random bunch of civilians into Marines. That requires training every aspect of a person: physical, mental, and moral. The transformation of hundreds of young men and women in thirteen weeks is mind-blowing. Making Marines is a heck of a mission. It's a testament to the value of focus, structure, effort, and commitment.

My platoon—2073, Golf Company, Second Battalion— came from different backgrounds all across the country. We were all colors. We were all faiths. Some were immigrants. English wasn't everyone's first language. Yet somehow, we were going to be molded into a group of people who could effectively act in unison. In thirteen weeks! I wouldn't have believed it was possible if I hadn't lived through it.

The physical challenges are only superficially difficult for most people. It's the other aspects of boot camp that end up being much harder. The drill instructors at boot camp trick you into focusing on the physical stuff. You don't even realize how much mental and moral growth occurs at the same time. The structures that work for you physically also work for you in other aspects of your life!

Every minute of every day in boot camp is planned out. There are no variables and no down time. Nothing to draw your attention away from the classes, the push-ups, the marching, or the shooting range. This ruthless focus is a necessary ingredient of boot camp. The drill instructors could not make Marines in thirteen weeks if they had to deal with outside distractions.

I didn't realize it at the time, but this was also my first exposure to the concept of iteration. Our drill instructors constantly pushed us to the edge. Then they backed off briefly to let us recover. And then they came back even harder! Again, and again, and again.

Like an entrepreneur steadily improving a business, our

platoon evolved from a hot mess of over 120 recruits into a tightly-knit tribe of eighty-five Marines.

The structure is unyielding. You eat, sleep, and breathe the values of the Corps: honor, courage, and commitment. Eventually, some part of you reawakens to the childhood fantasies of make-believe adventures. You too can be part of something great! You actually *can* become a Marine!

That's the moment when everything turns around. Things start to click. And the world gets a little better every day after that, buoyed up by your newfound confidence.

You are expected to accomplish a lot during boot camp, and things get tougher as you go along. There is a constant sense of growth, both individual and collective. You get better and better at a wide variety of things, all enabled by the demanding structure. This is part of the beauty of boot camp. Your identity is reshaped, slowly but surely, through the structure. Every day there is a new set of obstacles to overcome that are slightly harder than the ones from the day before. As we'll see in future chapters, confidence is the inevitable result of this kind of continuous training. It's a by-product of the action.

HIDDEN IN PLAIN SIGHT

The real surprise behind military training is there's a

new sense of personal accomplishment buried in all this structure. You are free from millions of details that might otherwise demand your attention.

Extreme focus and structure is a great way—maybe the only way—to systematically build confidence that sticks with you. The results from most programs go away when you leave the environment where it was developed. Over 90 percent of *The Biggest Loser* contestants regained the weight,[2] and some ended up even heavier than before!

Most of us will never go to boot camp, and that's fine. I wouldn't recommend it for everyone. But what we can take away from the military style of training is that a demanding daily routine can dramatically improve our abilities. It leads to an increase in confidence and builds momentum toward ever-greater accomplishments.

It's okay to start small. In fact, that's where we all start. The daily structure is the framework for our progression from beginner to expert. And that personal evolution is what eventually lets you enjoy the daily feeling of success.*

Jon noticed the exact same phenomenon in cities around the world. All these successful people had rigorous structures that propelled them forward. They were able to

---

* If this is what you need to hear, flip ahead to Chapter Fourteen and get some practical advice on how to build momentum.

repeat what worked for them over and over, getting better each time.

Structure provides freedom from distraction, a mental cushion. We need this space now, more than ever. Space to think. Space to explore. Space to ourselves.

Every single person who is connected to the digital world will benefit enormously from removing as many unneeded, superficial distractions as possible. Of course, that isn't exactly easy. The twenty-first century is the most difficult time in history if you want to stay focused on anything.

The digital world hates focus. Focus doesn't drive advertising revenue.

It's Miguel's birthday. Don't forget to say happy birthday! *Tap*. Check out this article. *Click*. Want to learn more? *Swipe*.

That's what those advertising companies want. More tapping, more clicking, and more swiping. Every time you succumb to a distraction, someone else makes money. And you lose focus on your mission.

Let's take advantage of structure to defeat the siren call of digital distractions. Let structure work for us and protect us against the endless stream of junk out there. Proper structure keeps us focused on all the incredible opportunities around us.

You are now ready to start building a successful life in the digital world. At this point in the book, you know about mental obesity, and how we're all choking on wave after wave of digital information. You know about the shortcomings of our traditional behaviors and education, and how it's preventing us from taking advantage of the opportunities around us. And you know about the core elements of a Reset: adopting the mission mentality, developing your bias toward action, and structuring your daily life.

Now you are about to embark on the most important part of the journey. In the next six chapters, we will learn to apply these principles in our daily lives.

◻—◻—◻

What to remember about "Structuring Success":

- Success is a daily practice of unusually effective behavior.
- The beginning is always small, but grows quickly.
- The right structure reinforces desirable behaviors, which builds confidence.
- Structure will improve you in physical, mental, and moral ways.

Take five minutes to consider the following questions:

- Do I have an unrealistic view of success?
- Am I regularly pushing myself to learn more and do more every day?
- What is an area I would love to improve in my life?
- Which daily patterns are holding me back?
- What is a simple switch I can make today to get me on track?

If you want to spend seven minutes learning more about the power of starting small with habitual changes, read "Get 1 Percent Better Every Day"[3] by Brett and Kate McKay.

If you want to spend five hours learning more about the importance of habits and personal transformation, read *The Power of Habit*[4] by Charles Duhigg.

PART IV

THE METHOD

CHAPTER TEN

SUPERCHARGE

WHAT IS THE MOST IMPORTANT MISTAKE I MAKE ALL THE TIME?

"If you spend your life trying to be good at everything, you will never be great at anything."

—TOM RATH, AMERICAN AUTHOR

My wife is an amazing person. She is an endless source of inspiration for me, both personally and professionally. She regularly does things that impress me with her capacity for love, wisdom, care, and optimism.

I learn a lot from my wife, even though I often reject each lesson the first time she tries to teach me. Or the second time. Or even the third!

A few years ago, the two of us were in Nigeria to run an entrepreneurial training program for GE called the Lagos Garage.[1]

We loved it. The program was the first of its kind: an immersive experience that combined the best aspects of the educational, vocational, and entrepreneurial approaches to economic development. We were there to unleash the creative energy of thousands of Nigerians who were building a brighter future for the country!

The Lagos Garage was an amazing experience for many reasons: the mission; the people; the location; and the culture. Most important, though, was that my wife and I ran the program together.

Even though the program was funded by GE, it was on a shoestring budget. We didn't mind, though, because we had this amazing mission! There was a never-ending stream of challenges, from intermittent electricity to aggressive building owners. A few days we weren't sure if the managers were going to let us stay in the classroom through the end of the program! Thank God my wife was there to smooth things over with people. Negotiating is one of her many talents, and definitely not one of mine.

One of my main responsibilities was to build the four-week curriculum. I drew heavily from my experiences in the Marines, Stanford, Singularity University, and as an entrepreneur myself.

Even though the curriculum and content had been finalized weeks before, I was never satisfied. I revisited every detail, thinking about things from every angle, then tweaking and rewriting many aspects of the programming.

The Lagos Garage was an experiment in a different way of training entrepreneurs. If—when—we were successful, GE would have a new model for supporting economic growth around the world.

My wife was preoccupied with other aspects of the program (for example, making sure we weren't kicked out of the building). But she was also going to help teach the entrepreneurs. This only made sense, since she is a Nigerian entrepreneur, and has an MBA from the Stanford Graduate School of Business.

She is also a total badass, which I think I already mentioned.

Despite all these factors, I stressed about her portion of the curriculum. Each day I'd start harassing her a few hours before the participants arrived. "Hey, you've got to start rehearsing what you're going to talk about today."

She would look up from her work and politely brush me off, saying, "Okay, honey, I'll take care of it." Then she would turn away and go back to whatever she was doing.

I would return to bug her every twenty or thirty minutes. She would smile and nod—her mouth tightening a bit each time—then keep doing what she was doing. The cycle repeated until it was ten minutes before the session was supposed to start.

And I'm *freaking* out by the end. I do not handle anxiety well. At all.

"What are you doing?" I would screech. "You're not prepared, and we start in five minutes. Almost everybody's here and you're not ready! The class is going to suck! The program is going to suck! Everything will suck, and we will *never* get to work on stuff like this again! Why are you trying to ruin this opportunity for me? I thought you loved me!"

Aren't you glad you aren't married to me?

SUPERWOMAN

When we finally kicked off each session with my wife's

opening remarks, she took effortless control of the room. She mesmerized the entire audience. People were on the edge of their seats. They could listen to her for hours on end, drawing insights and getting inspired to take their businesses to the next level.

My wife can have this level of impact on any group of people. Not only can she compel attention, she can also hold it for however long she wants. My wife is a charismatic person naturally, so when she actually tries to ramp up her energy, the result is nothing short of jaw-dropping. No one can touch her when she's in front of a group.

I still stressed out each day before we started. But during the third week, something finally clicked into place. I watched my wife in front of all these people, completely in her element. I realized I was watching someone who was world-class. Like, she's in the top 1 percent in the world when it comes to facilitation and teaching.

She knows exactly how to grab the room, to establish a deep connection with each and every person. Being onstage is so natural to her. She is in her environment, and she knows it. It's a beautiful thing to behold.

And then there's me. I go over the lesson plan dozens of times and still fall flat. People are slumping in their chairs, half asleep, or just on their phones.

That's pretty ridiculous if you think about it. After all, I *wrote* the lesson plan. These sessions should be a no-brainer for me, but I often struggle to connect with my audience. It takes hours of preparation for me to feel comfortable enough to bond with participants when I run a workshop or class. And the whole time I'm aware that my wife would do a much better job.

This was a frustrating experience for me in some ways. I have to admit I was a bit jealous. Okay, maybe *a lot* jealous.

But can you blame me? I want the satisfaction of being great. We all do. No one wants to end up with a thirteenth-place trophy. If we're honest with ourselves, most of us don't even want second place. We want to win. We want to be in first place. We want to be great!

What I learned from my wife was how we—starting with me—often channel energy into the wrong areas of our life.

POINTLESS COMPETITION

Developing unique skills is a key challenge and opportunity in the creative economy. Think about the power we can unlock with this approach.

Take the time to seriously consider this question: "Can I take my natural talents and work hard with other talented people to develop something that is uniquely valuable to other people?"

That was the revelation my wife demonstrated to me for weeks before I really understood it. Don't try to balance yourself out. Supercharge yourself!

If you maximize your strengths, then your weaknesses will become irrelevant. And the power of your strengths will attract other people to complement you. Your world-class effectiveness will inspire others to take it to the next level. Or several levels! That sort of beneficial dynamic guarantees your value and theirs.

Choosing mediocrity, by contrast, means choosing a life defined by insecurity. You can replace average, but you can't replace great.

IF YOU CAN'T BEAT 'EM...

Peter Thiel, billionaire entrepreneur and investor, dealt with a near-fatal business situation early in his career when he was building the financial services company, PayPal. Elon Musk, another now-famous Silicon Valley entrepreneur, was working on a similar company called X.com. The two entrepreneurs and their companies fought each other viciously at first, but they wised up after a year or so.

Rather than trying to destroy each other, they decided to combine forces and leverage the unique strengths of each company.[2] The resulting partnership was incredibly successful. The new and improved PayPal grew even faster, and it was purchased by eBay in 2002 for $1.4 billion.

The same principle holds true in the much smaller activities. It's not just about business. My wife and I know to separate cooking—her job—from setting the table and washing the dishes—my job. If we didn't play to our strengths, we would end up with bad food and dirty dishes.

THE FLAW OF AVERAGES

Don't strive to be the average of all the things you can do. Instead, focus on the things you do really well. Those activities will most likely fulfill you and ultimately will have the largest positive impact on others.

Positive impact through daily actions is how we should define success in the digital world. As we learned in the last chapter, success is not just another word for rich, or some abstract goal for the future. Success is the daily practice of positive impact on others. These daily practices are ideally based on our specific strengths.

Supercharging yourself is one of the first steps to a successful life. Why? Because we can only be consistently impactful—and rewarded for that impact—in areas where we become masters. Areas where we are unusually good. And that level of skill and confidence only results from developing our strengths to an uncommon degree.

Achieving mastery lets us tap into both the analytic and creative parts of our souls. Mastery sustains us through difficult periods where we don't get the financial or social rewards we had expected. We learn to embrace the process and not get distracted with worldly outcomes. You're doing this for you, after all.

Mastery breeds confidence like nothing else. That's the power of repetition and results. No one can take away that confidence once it takes root. Someone's opinion holds no weight compared to what you know you can do.

Mastery also frees us to focus on the impact we have on other people, not just ourselves. Over time, we stop being self-conscious. With practice, our unique skills become extensions of us. Our ego can fade into the background. The results speak for themselves.

We become masters through a combination of two things: natural ability and dedicated practice. You might think practice is the harder part, but actually, most of us cannot clearly identify our natural abilities. We often try to develop the wrong skills because we don't get enough critical feedback from people around us.

Most people have a hard time with this concept. I'm saying that it's almost impossible for us to identify when we're not good at something. Why? Because we were taught to do the exact *opposite* in school. Refer to Chapter Two if you need a refresher on all the ways we are led down the wrong path in traditional school classrooms.

EDUCATIONAL MALWARE

Would you call someone a good student if they showed you their report card and it had three A's and three F's? Of course not! That's a C average. No one is shooting for a C average.

But that is how the creative economy works. Averages don't matter. Focus on the areas where you are talented, then find people who make your weaknesses irrelevant. Someone could have one A and five F's and still be very successful!

It's time to reprogram our minds. We have to discard that old industrial-age mindset of basic competence in a wide range of skills. Human beings are not Swiss Army

Knives: sort of useful in some situations. That flawed way of thinking is holding us back.

We need to stop labeling the areas where we struggle as "bad" and other areas as "good." No one should be striving to be "good" at everything. Weak points are actually opportunities for collaboration!

In the creative economy, we will be rewarded for our ability to attract people with complementary skills. We want to build these people into a coalition of willing members who want to work together and solve a problem of common interest.*

How can we start acting in line with this revelation? First, we need to identify these opportunities for collaboration. And that means we have to figure out where we can use a bit of help.

STARTING POINT

Like most people, your abilities fall on a bell-shaped curve. Think of a camel's hump. It starts skinny on one end, grows fatter toward the middle, and then gets skinny again. The skinny part on the left represents your abilities that are truly horrible. As the curve gets fatter toward the middle, you are progressing into areas where you are...not terrible.

---

* That's a pretty good definition of a company, by the way.

The big fat middle represents all those abilities where you are average. You're one of the crowd, which is totally fine. Then you proceed into the skinny end at the right where you are good, great, and finally, world class.

We've been trained to pay attention to the big fat middle. Don't do that! The skinny parts—the extreme abilities—are where things get interesting. Other people sit up and take notice when you engage in these activities. Sometimes that is because you suck and are embarrassing yourself. Other times, it's because you are crushing it.

That positive extreme is your sweet spot. Your zone of potential mastery. This is where you can become truly world-class. You can supercharge!

The tricky part is mapping out this curve. You don't want to invest a bunch of time and energy into activities where you can only be pretty good. You should be aiming for mastery.

Only a lucky few can objectively assess ourselves, though. The rest of us have a hard time gaining perspective on something as personal as our God-given abilities. Many of us hang on to impressions from our past. It's like someone trying desperately to convince everyone that she is a great writer because a tenth grade English teacher once gave her an "A-" on an essay.

This is where the bias toward action will come in handy. Don't start identifying strengths by thinking. Go do things! Do things you haven't done before.

Do more intense versions of things you've already done.

Do the same thing with more people.

Do the same thing with different people.

THE GIFT THAT KEEPS ON GIVING

Taking action gives you the greatest gift anyone can receive: feedback. It is impossible to understand where you fall on the spectrum without feedback. This is why engaging in a wide variety of activities is the best place to start. You only get feedback after you try lots of stuff.

Feedback is useful because it clumps at the extreme ends of the spectrum. You will receive feedback about the activities where you are terrible and the activities where you are great.

You won't get feedback in most instances, though. Average experiences do not prompt people to take time to tell you what they think. You're not going to get an email from somebody after a meeting that says, "Hey, that was pretty average. Okay, talk to you later."

Someone's either going to say, "Man, you tanked. What happened?" or, "Wow, that was amazing. You did a great job!"

This feedback is priceless to someone who wants to be world class. It's the best approach to identifying opportunities to supercharge. You take action, you listen for feedback, and then you improve based on what you heard. Act, listen, improve.

This is the individual version of Silicon Valley's Minimum Viable Product that we already learned about. The difference here is you are your own MVP. The key concept is to learn and improve, not fall in love with yourself as you are right now.

You are version 1.0 and are only going to get better.

With each cycle of action and feedback, you will get closer to your true potential. Each bit of feedback is a sign pointing you in the right direction, a gift from someone to help you find your way. A clue to a future you!

With enough feedback, you can be confident in areas of potential mastery based on evidence. It's not just you trying to become a great designer because you read a cool article about design, or because you like to wear thick-framed glasses in black or red. No, you are pursuing specific areas thanks to a sturdy foundation of people telling you what they loved and what they hated.

EMOTIONAL RADAR

Listening to feedback isn't the only way to identify potential areas of mastery. You can also pay attention to your emotions. Look for moments when you see another person doing something and think, "I can do better than *that*!" These are points where the creativity inside you bubbles up. You spontaneously imagine yourself excelling in that activity. Again, this is a clue to the parts of your life where you can stand out. That emotional connection indicates you will be willing to prove that you can excel through months or years of work.

Back in 2012, I watched two people run an interactive simulation developed by a company called ExperiencePoint.[3] This pair of designers were exposing a large group to the core principles of Design Thinking: observe people, form insights about their behavior, brainstorm solutions, and rapidly test those solutions with cheap experiments.

It was a fascinating session, and I studied the facilitators intently. I paid attention to their body language, tone of voice, and dynamics with the audience. And I decided on the spot that I could do this better than the guys I was watching, even though they were professionals.

These guys were doing something very different than my wife. She can carry a group with sheer charisma, but this session was designed for another purpose. With ExperiencePoint, the goal is to distill complex concepts into simple, digestible information via interactive group work. To connect the dots between the experience of the participants during the session to their day-to-day work. The participants are being taught the mechanics and language of Design Thinking, which we talked about in Chapter Eight.

This kind of facilitation was right up my alley. So, I worked on my facilitation skills for several years, doing free work whenever I could to further develop my skills. And, of course, I got a lot of feedback. Because I sucked at the beginning.

In 2014, I was referred to ExperiencePoint by a friend. I jumped at the chance to get certified and have since run sessions for all kinds of organizations across the country. I also applied these skills in my own businesses as they grew and took on a life of their own!

What a confidence-building feeling, to go from nothing to an expert, and all based on a feeling! It was impossible to ignore, like I was being *pulled* toward something. And I had no previous experience with anything like it before. All I knew was, "I can do that better."

That's a clue, so pay attention to it. Listen to your soul. The activities that appeal to you, however unlikely they seem, could be something on which you build a successful career.

THE "SORT OF" TRAP

"But what about all those things I *sort of* like?" you might ask. "I've always thought it would be *sort of* cool to [insert random dream here]."

I hope I don't lose you with my response, but I can't lie to you. Ignore that stuff. Run away from all your *sort of* dreams!

Seriously, push all those thoughts out of your mind. Throw away all those lukewarm fantasies. They don't matter. All the stuff you *kind of* want to do should be avoided at all costs.

Highly focused and purpose-driven people know this. This is part of the feedback process we discussed in the last chapter, where Jessica paid close attention to which of her daily actions led to the desired outcome. She had to be ruthlessly focused on the stuff that worked *and* appealed to her. Both boxes must be checked.

Warren Buffett asks his employees to write down a list of

their top twenty-five goals. The first five items go on their to-do list. The next twenty items become the Avoid-at-All-Costs List.[4] The lesson? Only go for what truly matters because life will inevitably distract you. That advice is even more important in the digital world.

The time you spend on things you *kind of* want to do will strangle your true dreams. The digital world will dangle those opportunities in front of you all the time. Ignore them. You want to be on fire for your goals.

This is a tough process, and it isn't for the faint of heart. Fortunately, you don't need to go through the supercharging process alone. Think of your close friends and family. People who know you well. What would they say if you asked them about the activities where you truly excel? You might get a variety of responses in terms of details, but there will be unmistakable trends. A few of your strengths will rise to the top.

Be prepared for surprising feedback. Your friends may identify strengths that don't align with the way you think about yourself. You may have imagined yourself doing very different things to have an impact in the world.

Try not to get hung up with the details right now. The key to supercharging is giving yourself permission to become great. You are creating space to progress toward mastery.

And no one ever said mastery was easy. That's why we need help!

⊡—⊡—⊡

What you need to remember about "Supercharge":

- Focus on your strengths and don't try to even yourself out.
- Enlist the help of other people who complement your strengths.
- Focus your efforts on a few things that you desperately want to do.
- Pay attention to the feedback you get from other people.

Actions that require less than ten minutes:

- Write yourself an email with the subject, "My Legacy" that lists the names of ten family and friends you can survey to determine your greatest strengths. Continue by listing five fun activities you need to avoid because they are used as distractions from focusing on your greatest strengths.

Actions that require less than thirty minutes:

- Write down your own version of Warren Buffett's Top

Twenty-Five list. Circle the top five and then write a date next to each of them to indicate when (the month and year) you want to complete it. Then identify the skills you will need to accomplish each goal, plus a teacher you can use and a student who will help along the way.

- Make a list of ten activities where you get positive feedback from other people, or where you get that "I can do that better!" feeling. Go through the list scoring each activity on a one-to-ten scale, with ten being something you love doing every day no matter what.

Actions that require an hour or more:

- Send out a survey to trustworthy friends and family with your top ten activities list. Ask them for their honest opinion of whether they think you should pursue any of these, and why or why not. Analyze the results by grouping useful feedback into areas of potential mastery. Consider your life if you pursued each activity. What would your day look like? Who could you talk to that does that now?
- If you are willing to be more open about this, put up the same survey on Facebook or your favorite social media community. Ask the same questions and follow up with people individually if they respond.

CHAPTER ELEVEN

RALLY

AM I SUPPOSED TO BE DOING ALL THIS MYSELF?

"But he that is greatest among you shall be your servant."
—BOOK OF MATTHEW, CHAPTER 23, VERSE 11, KING JAMES BIBLE

My whole body was on fire when I woke up on September 2, 2000. I had moved into a new apartment the day before, trying to Reset my life. Out with the bad, in with the good.

Part of the process was physical fitness. I needed to lose weight, so I could enlist in the Marine Corps. And so, on the first night at my new place, I had gone for my very first jog. Ever.

That was a huge mistake, or at least it felt like one. My entire body ached, all six-foot-four and 300 pounds of it. My ankles hurt. My calves hurt. My knees hurt. My hips hurt. Even my toenails hurt, which I didn't even know was possible until that moment.

My mission of losing weight to become a Marine was put to the test. No one told me it was going to feel like this, especially not on the second day!

I had to figure out if I would go for another jog that evening or admit defeat. I don't mean to blow this out of proportion. That was how it *felt*. If I couldn't jog two nights in a row, how could I hope to make it through boot camp?

Fortunately, I was an eighteen-year-old male. Or, to put it less charitably, I was stubborn and full of pride. And testosterone.

So I called on that amazing supply of youthful energy. I stumbled out for a jog that evening. And then again the next evening. And the next, and the next, and the next. I jogged every evening for months on end until the habit of physical exercise was seared into my soul.

And I did it all alone.

Trying to go through this whole process by myself was

misguided and ultimately unnecessary. I should have involved my family and friends. I should have enjoyed myself more. But I didn't know what else to do except throw blood, sweat, and tears at my mission. The only thing I knew how to do was grind.

This type of silent struggle is common. Common and stupid. The "lone hero" approach is a flawed strategy. For every publicized example of people changing their lives through sheer willpower, there are dozens or hundreds of failures.[*] Yet, the image of one person doing it alone is a core theme of American culture.

STRONGER TOGETHER

So many of us live a long life and yet end up dying with our greatness trapped inside. Why? Because ability to realize our potential is based on three profound truths:

1. Most major outcomes in life are determined by our daily habits.
2. We tend to isolate ourselves when attempting to change those habits.
3. We usually quit within one month.

We quit for lots of reasons, and many of them are pretty good. It's harder than we thought, so we quit. We get

---

[*] It's called survivorship bias: https://en.wikipedia.org/wiki/Survivorship_bias

distracted, so we quit. Someone was mean or unfair, so we quit.

Obstacles are real. We have to face them anytime we try to accomplish something meaningful. But obstacles are also surmountable. To be successful, we have to try a different approach, one that helps us keep going despite the unavoidable trials.

The key is recognizing we cannot sustain anything alone. It is both easier and more enjoyable to maintain our enthusiasm through the love and support of the people around us. Rally your crew and you are much more likely to realize your dreams!

This is where a compelling mission reenters the picture. Remember the insight from Chapter Seven? An inspiring mission with a powerful *Why?* and *Who?* will attract support from your friends.

This social support might be obvious, or it might be unexpected. It might be immediate, or it might be delayed. But it will emerge. Friends will pop up out of nowhere when you're trying to do anything worthwhile. You will be blown away by the amount of valuable assistance others will offer.

There are three groups of people we need to pursue for a meaningful life over the long term: teachers, students, and cheerleaders. We need each group if we want to reach our destination, and if we want to enjoy the journey. The relationships will build, deepen, and propel us forward in the good times, and drag us forward in the bad times.

These groups represent your own personal tribe, the people who are there for you when it matters. It's critical for you to understand each group: what they do, why you need them, and who might belong to it.

TEACHERS

Teachers offer immediate help because they just went through the same thing and have the scars to prove it. A teacher is a tool. You share a practical and pragmatic connection with this person. Your relationship with each teacher should revolve around learning something specific and useful. You might have teachers for five years or five minutes. It depends on how long you both find the relationship useful.

This is a symbiotic relationship. The value to the teacher is the deepening of his or her knowledge. Both people should be improving. The student is getting way better at the basics and application of a particular skill. The teacher is getting better too, by clarifying the true utility and purpose of the skill.

Of course, I'm not talking about the teacher who stands at

the front of a classroom. I'm also not talking about a grey-haired mentor who descends from their lofty perch to offer divine wisdom. No Yodas and no condescending lectures.

You need a teacher who is in the trenches with you. Think "player coach." They may only be a few steps ahead of you, not necessarily an established expert. Many of them are more like accomplished peers than anything else.

It's essential that teachers are honest. This is no time for coddling egos. As we've discussed in earlier chapters, blunt feedback speeds up your rate of learning, maximizing the value of your time together. This might seem counter-intuitive, but you cannot let your teacher off easy. You want to be demanding of the teacher just like you expect a good teacher to be demanding of you.

Top universities are already moving to this style of collaborative learning. My friend Bill, a mechanical engineering lecturer at Stanford, teaches the world's best class on designing innovative products.[1] He is always looking for new ways to engage meaningfully with students because they already have access to the class material. Most of them show up to the first day of class having watched all the lectures!

Bill's role as a teacher is changing. He is no longer the gatekeeper for the information. There is only one approach he can take that's actually useful to the students. He needs to help them apply the curriculum to their specific area of interest. He is a guide, not a god.

Each person walks into class with a list of questions and then walks out a few hours later with a list of stuff to do. That is being a teacher in a true sense. Bill is guiding them toward action and the deep, significant learning that comes with it.

STUDENTS

This is someone with whom you can share lessons from your own journey. In this case, the teacher is you. You are the person who is a few steps ahead, helping someone else walk the path.

The focus must be practical wisdom. Students don't need a pep talk. No dramatic music in the background. No blue face paint *a la* Mel Gibson in *Braveheart*. What they need is momentum to get them past that critical early period when they are starting to do something new. You should be pointing out specific tasks they need to accomplish or angles they need to consider.

"Make sure you take a jacket and a bottle of water."

"Okay, now wait for them to respond to your email before writing back."

"Did you remember to save a copy for your records?"

Remember, you are not the person with all the answers. You are the person trying to push the student to learn through action. You are useful to the student because they're facing a situation that is similar to something in your past.

Being a teacher is incredibly fulfilling, but it is also useful. As you teach, you remind yourself of key principles and models. It's a reminder of all the wisdom you've gained over the years, even if you don't always apply it. You are improving your own knowledge and skills while helping out someone else. Developing these types of relationships is a powerful reminder of how much you know that is useful to others, and how easy it is to have a positive impact on someone else.

A TEACHER IN ACTION

My uncle Craig helped a woman do her homework and it literally changed her life. He was a student majoring in mathematics at Southern Oregon University. One day as Craig was leaving the library, he walked by a young woman whom he recognized from one of his classes. She was sitting on a bench doing her homework, and she was clearly stressed out.

Craig stopped to say hi briefly, then stayed to help her

work through one or two problems. He was on his way within five minutes.

That was it. Craig never gave it another thought until twenty years later when that woman approached him at a college reunion. She told him that on that day she was so frustrated that she had decided to drop out of college. But when he walked her through the solutions to a few tough problems, she was encouraged to stay and finish school.

That short break to help do her homework ended up saving her college career and setting her up for professional success!

And it wasn't just about the woman. That story ended up having a huge impact on my uncle more than twenty years after the fact. Since the reunion, he regularly thinks back to that day in the library.

It's a concrete reminder to him about the power of small gestures. How they can motivate us to keep going, no matter what.

That's what happens when you teach others, even in a way that doesn't seem important to you at the time. You're dropping a stone in a pond. There are positive ripples that expand from that action. Whether any of them get back to you is not the point. You can be confident the ripples will reach someone.

CHEERLEADERS

This last group of folks is here to remind you that you're not alone. They send you a nice email when you reach an important milestone. They grab a cup of coffee and listen to you talk about a frustrating situation. They offer important feedback about a situation where you're not operating at your best.

My grandfather, a veteran of both World War II and the Korean War, wrote me four letters during boot camp. He knew exactly what I needed to hear during those thirteen weeks. And you better believe I read and reread those letters until I had them memorized.

Cheerleaders are like training wheels or crutches. They keep you from falling over. They bridge that crucial gap between the time when you start something new and the time you start seeing the benefits. Cheerleaders function best with little opportunities to give you a "Hey, good job" text or email. That's what friends are for.

Everyone needs this sort of positive reinforcement. We are social animals, as we saw by digging into the distorted lens of social media in Chapter Three. There's a huge emotional benefit when you can sense you are having an impact on others. That's why we care so much when other people share their intimate experiences with us.

Teachers, students, and cheerleaders can help us accomplish incredible feats while enjoying the daily work that gets us there. To construct a fulfilling life, we need to learn to effectively use these three groups.

I wish I had understood the value of these groups back in 2000 when I was getting in shape for the Marines, or in 2005, when I went back to community college in hopes of earning a degree.

Every time I did something hard, my default approach was to do it on my own. I kept my family and friends at a distance instead of inviting them to support me. I muscled through the difficult initial phase. "Embrace the suck" is an informal motto of the Marine Corps. And that's just what I did—embraced the suck—over and over and over again.

It wasn't until 2008 when I first reached out to others for advice, and began offering it in return. After a deployment to Iraq, I returned to campus and started counseling other veterans who were attending nearby community colleges. This helped them transfer to better four-year universities while keeping my own skills sharp.

Getting veterans to apply to better top-tier universities became a mission for me. I knew they could compete with elite prep school students, but I had to figure out how to get them to believe it, too. So I worked with Dr. Jess Matthews—then the Associate Dean of Stanford Summer Session—to create a program to help enlisted veterans come to Stanford for the summer, free of charge.[2] Now called 2 to 4: A Veteran's Accelerator, the program has transformed the lives of dozens of student veterans, with hundreds more coming through in the future.

The veterans who attend 2 to 4 have a life-changing experience, but that's only part of the mission. All the alumni return to their community colleges to spread the gospel to their fellow veterans. They go from being students to teachers in a few months. And their support of other veterans will reinforce the lessons they need to apply in their own lives.

That's the essence of rallying people.

GIFT THAT KEEPS ON GIVING

Imagine how different life can be if you tap into these groups of people to help you with a compelling mission. You will be able find and engage fascinating experts in whichever areas interest you. You will be able to develop a wider range of skills more quickly and enjoy your work. You will be able to feel the satisfaction of helping others. And you will know without a doubt your life is having a positive impact on this world.

This is true for any kind of work that focuses on other people, no matter the job. You could be a graphic designer, a firefighter, a pet store owner, a fashion blogger, whatever. It doesn't matter. You will be better at what you do, and you will enjoy your life more if you find simple ways to help others.

Rallying a crucial part of your Reset. Your decision to take control of your life can become the inspiration for others.

You probably know dozens—maybe hundreds—of people who are trying to motivate themselves to take that first step. They want to change their lives, too. Your Reset can help push them over the edge into sustained, powerful action. It could be your encouragement or advice propelling them toward a life of true freedom. To say *No!* to distractions of the world. To create something beautiful, valuable, and meaningful.

Imagine giving someone else that kind of gift. It's in your power. And you have no idea how good it will feel until you see the look of appreciation in someone's face. Of course, we need to start somewhere. And here again are powerful lessons from the strangely parallel worlds of the military and Silicon Valley.

Whether the goal is defending a nation or building a business, your rate of learning needs to be incredibly high.

Both environments are full of risks and threats as well as opportunities. Your job is to sort through all the stuff flying at you and take decisive action as quickly as possible. There is no time for endless conversations about the fine print. You need to create an environment where people are constantly sharing practical information. Fortunately, that is precisely what you will do.

RALLYING CRY

The military has a rich tradition of "hip pocket" classes. These are short, informal periods of instruction that teach a specific skill or address a specific deficiency to a small group of people. The concept is deceptively simple: someone knows how to do something that a lot of other people don't know how to do, so that person teaches everybody else how to do it.*

The teacher—the person who knows the skill—gets everyone in a circle. He or she quickly describes the situation where the training is useful, before diving into the skill itself. Then a few random people are asked to demonstrate or summarize the class for everyone else. This usually takes between five and fifteen minutes depending on the topic and number of questions. Fast but effective.

The entrepreneurial equivalent to a hip pocket class is

---

* Here's a fantastic example for machine gunners: https://imgur.com/zxz4xyo

called an *unconference*.[3] I first saw this when I was working at Singularity University in 2011.[4] An unconference is a peer-based learning session that usually lasts about a half day. The attendees propose classes they are willing to teach.

Say there are three classrooms and five different time slots. That's fifteen classes. You create a three-by-five matrix on a wall, so the participants can sign up under each available class time. People then pitch their workshop idea to everyone else. Everyone votes on their favorites—usually each person gets three votes—and the most popular workshops get taught.

Through unconferences, I've attended world-class workshops on foreign languages by a Turkish woman who spoke thirteen languages, a session on investing in private markets by an incredibly successful British banker, and another on strategic decision-making by a Fortune 500 executive.

Fascinating stuff, all of it for free, and none of it had to be pre-planned. Like hip pocket classes, an unconference is powered by our natural desire to share knowledge with others in practical ways.

Why do these practices work so well? They take advantage of our social nature. We learn much better from our peers than anyone else because there is a free flow of information and a natural similarity of perspective. A sixty-year-old teacher can't connect well to a twenty-year-old student, especially when the communication is as one-sided as your traditional classroom environment.

To protect ourselves from the digital world's constant distractions, we need constant, practical connections to our friends and family. These collaborative engagements will protect and inspire us as we charge through each day. And that takes us directly into our next topic.

Generating the daily momentum that will help us accomplish our missions in life.

□—□—□

What to remember about "Rally":

- Involving other people maximizes your chance of success in any activity.
- Find teachers, people who can help you learn a specific skill.
- Find students, people who need to learn something you can teach them.
- Find cheerleaders, people who want to encourage you in a specific activity.
- Learn from those around you, like in the examples of the military's hip pocket class or Silicon Valley's unconference.

Actions that require less than five minutes:

- Write yourself an email with the subject, "My Support" that lists one possible teacher, one possible student, and one possible cheerleader. Add a brief note after each name explaining what you will do for them, and/ or what you would like them to do for you.

Actions that require less than thirty minutes:

- Identify something specific you need to learn for work or school, then find a friend who knows how to do it. Email that person and ask them to spend a few minutes on the phone or in person to discuss the topic. At the end of the conversation, ask them if there is any way you can reciprocate.

Actions that require a few hours or more:

- Pick a topic that interests you, anything from motorcycle racing to French cooking. Set a date over a weekend at least two months in the future. Contact a small group of friends and coworkers who are interested in the same topic, asking them to join you for a few hours. Propose specific sessions that would be useful and find someone who knows enough to teach it.

CHAPTER TWELVE

LAUNCH

WHAT'S THE MOST IMPORTANT CHANGE TO MAKE?

*"Lose an hour in the morning, and you
will spend all day looking for it."*

—RICHARD WHATLEY, BRITISH THEOLOGIAN

Have you ever seen a Japanese tea ceremony?* It is beautiful. You can't help but relax as you watch the person go through the choreography. Every movement is so controlled and precise. There is a proper place for everything: the person's hands, the tray, the napkin, the cup. All of it carefully orchestrated and harmonious.

---

* You can watch one here: https://www.youtube.com/watch?v=lL9BiNuImws

We all live in a world of rituals—glorified habits—like the Japanese tea ceremony, whether or not we realize it. Generations ago, we followed the same rituals as other people in our tribe, religion, and nation. We could recognize when other people were engaging in rituals. We accepted these rituals as a part of our lives, and they helped bind us together. We understood their power to center us, guide us, and infuse the world with meaning.

People don't share many rituals anymore. We have fewer common experiences. What's left are the habits we choose for ourselves, but that no one else can recognize.

Replacing communal rituals with individual habits is a problem. We take rituals much more seriously. Rituals can help make the difference between a distracted life and one filled with purpose, impact, and community. That is why it's critical for you to develop rituals to help you begin each day properly. Specifically, you will need to develop rituals that reinforce your purpose. We need to own the beginning of each day.

Our goal is to be unleashed on an unsuspecting world. We should want to erupt out of bed! And to accomplish that, we need to make the late evening and the early morning *sacred*. It should be a special time when you are able to pursue your priorities without the noise and confusion of the digital world.

In short, you need to learn to launch yourself.

THE LAUNCHPAD

To launch is to clarify success. You will develop a clear picture of what you're doing, the outcome you're expecting from each action, and the people who will benefit as a result. You know when you are starting and when you are finished. You are not compelled to lurch from task to task, working on someone else's priorities. Instead, you will be on fire for your own work.

To launch is to take unapologetic ownership of your day. When you launch, you are carving out space in your schedule to do one thing: generate momentum toward accomplishing a short list of critical tasks. After tackling these few important things, you get to ease into the rest of the day, brimming with confidence from your early wins.

Think back to your last few workdays. Did you start your day or just stumble into it? Did your work have an impact on anyone or was it swallowed up into a black hole? Were you in meetings and reading emails because they were important or because they were on your schedule? Did you know when you were done with your important work or did you just sort of coast to a stop?

Most of us have pretty depressing answers to these questions. By now, you should know it's not our fault, even though the responsibility still lies with us. Think about the rapid intrusion of the digital world. We have to dodge distractions like never before, and the range of options in front of us can be paralyzing if we're not careful.

No one ever said Resetting was going to be easy. It's not supposed to be, at least not at first. But launching is the most effective daily method for living with purpose.

We don't have perfect control over our day. That's impossible. There are endless responsibilities that need to be addressed. And the digital world is always lurking, ready to swallow up any free time with bright and shining distractions.

Are these obstacles going to be in our way? Of course. That's precisely why you need to Reset. Life in the digital world is all about setting and pursuing your priorities, not anyone else's.

DO-GOODER

Benjamin Franklin, probably the most interesting and certainly the most commercially successful of the Founding Fathers, was a master of this sort of daily launch. He was famous for his simple yet profound question, "What good shall I do this day?"[1] That was his way of orienting and channeling all his efforts.

Franklin knew that beginnings are special. And the beginning of each day is no exception. You are distanced from the successes and the failures of the previous day. Your soul is healed after those little traumas and sadnesses that accumulate from dawn to dusk. In short, you should be ready to stride confidently into the world.

Except that we rarely feel that way. Most of us do not launch into the day. Instead, we stumble into it. We *lurch* into it. Most days start as an embarrassment of muddy confusion.

Can you guess why? Ask yourself, "What is the last thing we do before we go to sleep?" Check our phones, of course. "And what is the first thing most of us do when we wake up?" Again, check our phones.

The result of these choices should be no surprise. We swipe from distraction to distraction, never building purpose, momentum, or a sense of satisfaction.

Why? Because when we default to plugging into the digital world, we lose a sense of direction. Now we are doing what other people want us to do. When you check email, you are reading through a list of things other people need you to accomplish. When you check social media, you are reading through a list of things that other people need you to care about.

At this point in the book, you should be confident there is never a shortage of people who want you to do things for them. Family. Friends. Marketers. Everyone. But what about the actions that align with our goals? Who is responsible for making sure we make time for what matters to us?

That would be you. You and you alone. Creating a life that rises to this occasion requires preparation. It requires discipline. It requires a Reset.

US VERSUS THEM

Let's be very clear about why launching is such a critical habit. On any given day, you are going to do one of two things: what you want to do, or what other people want you to do.

It's binary. It is one or the other. You can only accomplish one thing at a time—your goals, or other people's goals. Because no one else has specific daily goals that overlap perfectly with yours. They want what they want. You want what you want.

Even if other people truly want to see you succeed in your goals, they are too busy dealing with their own life to consistently put you back on track. So, it all comes back to you.

Only one of these choices—doing what you want—will

lead to a fulfilling life. You need to be ruthless about pursuing these goals. It's basically impossible to start the day doing work for others and then go back to start working on your own priorities. You have to get it right out of the gate.

Of course, there are times when you absolutely need to do what other people want you to do. That's what it means to be an employee, spouse, parent, sibling, or friend.

Life is complicated. But that doesn't excuse you from the responsibility of carving out the time to accomplish your mission. That's part of taking full responsibility for building the life you want.

Resist the temptation to start coming up with excuses right now. Yes, you have to deal with a lot of drama at work. Yes, your family takes up a lot of your time. Yes, you are not getting enough sleep. These are all true. True, and yet irrelevant at the same time.

This will sound harsh, condescending, or both. But...get over it. And not because I said that you need to. Get over it because if you don't, you will find yourself in the same place in fifteen or twenty years. And if you were satisfied right now, you wouldn't be reading this.

Remember, everyone has the same twenty-four hours in

a day. Some of us just use those hours more wisely, and we both want you to become one of those people.

SLEEP TIGHT

Hopefully, we can now agree that developing momentum—launching—is a great way to start each day. So how do you do it? In a perfect world, launching begins the night before. You don't just wake up knowing exactly what you're supposed to do that day. You must take the time to connect in a deep and profound way to your priorities for the next day.

All it takes is one minute. Before you head to bed, write down the major tasks you need to accomplish the next day, making sure to indicate the most important one. That's the first thing you will tackle when you begin work.

This practice is incredibly powerful if you stick with it. Yes, it will clarify your goals for the following day, which is valuable. But writing down a list also helps your brain prepare for sleep. There is an inherent sense of relief and relaxation from knowing you won't forget any of the important stuff you need to do.

Your list should be no longer than five items. Any more than that and you are writing down details that don't really matter. The goal is to stay focused on the activities that align with your mission in a fundamental way.

Groceries don't make the cut.

Once you're done, put the list on top of your phone. I mean that literally. You should actually place the list on top of your phone, so you can't see the screen. Your list is a physical barrier between you and the digital world. It should remind you about what's important when you wake up the next morning.

While you're at it, go plug in your phone at the most convenient outlet that is near the front door. That will keep you safely away from any distractions at both the end and beginning of every day. If you need an alarm clock to wake up, go buy a regular one.* Putting away your phone is the beginning of cleansing your environment. It's a great way to restructure your world in a way that gives you some space. We'll dig more into this in the next chapter.

So you've made two small adjustments to your nightly ritual: moved your phone out of your bedroom, and written a to-do list with no more than five items. Simple enough. One minute of work, and you've earned yourself a better night's rest.

---

*   It's just $15 and it will be delivered to your door in a few days: http://www.amazon.com/gp/product/B00IEYHMIM

Do not head straight to your phone after you wake up. I can't stress this enough. Both your list and the phone will be there, waiting for you when you're actually ready to start the day.

Instead, you will do the simplest, most basic, and most helpful thing you can do. You are going to make your bed. I stumbled on this practice through my military training, but I've seen how much of a difference it makes for the people who adopt the practice.

Admiral William McRaven—who happens to be a Navy SEAL—stressed the importance of making your bed in a 2014 commencement address to the University of Texas. "If you do so, it will mean that the first thing you do in the morning is to accomplish something, which sets the tone for the day, encourages you to accomplish more, and reinforces that little things matter."[2] Those are three compelling reasons, and they tie directly into the importance of reinforcing our mindset through daily action.

There is a complementary ritual you also need to adopt: tidying up your home. Basic clean-up after you wake up helps us prepare for decluttering the day that lies ahead. You are removing the debris in both cases, creating space for what truly matters.

I'm not asking for much. Pick up any clothes on the floor,

put away toiletries that are strewn across the bathroom sink, and wash any dishes in the sink. Two or three minutes, max.

You will find that your mind naturally starts to wander as you tidy. You start thinking about all the stuff you could do that day, which is great. Daydreaming is exactly what you want, because it mimics the distractions of the digital world. You don't need to worry about being too focused yet, because your to-do list is waiting for you, on top of your phone where you left it.

THE WHO

Now is your time to deepen the level of commitment to each task on that list. Your goal is to remind yourself why it's so important to accomplish this specific goal. Think about the people whose lives will benefit and how you will feel as a result. This is the *Who?* and *Why?* from the mission mentality that pairs so nicely with the *What?* of the to-do list.

This works even for the boring work stuff. At night, I may write down something I need to do, such as "Send end-of-month report to client." This is the sort of mundane task that normally drives me crazy. But in the morning, I scribble the outcome to the right of the task that says, "So the client sees all the great work we're doing, is confident about the project, and looks forward to the final result."

Beyond the inspirational value, this process also ensures that each item is worthy of the list. If you can't clearly explain the *Who?* and *Why?* you should remove that item. Remember, this list is the fuel for your launch. You will get distracted if you aren't driven to accomplish these tasks.

Try it for one week. Start with one item on your to-do list. Just one simple, important thing you want to accomplish the next day. You'll be amazed at how much it can motivate you.

A POWERFUL BLEND

Consider how we are blending the Mission Mentality, Success Structure, and Bias Toward Action in these chapters. Each concept is your tool to deny the petty requests that bombard you every day, but they help you get fired up about the truly meaningful work in your life. You are joining the likes of Benjamin Franklin by trying to answer the question, "What good shall I do this day?"

You are now ready. There are no hurdles left before you can begin to fulfill your daily purpose. Your priorities are burned into your mind. You can picture the rest of the day. You have successfully prepared yourself for taking action that connects deeply to you and the people you care about.

Now we have to make sure we can accomplish our priorities before the digital world gets us to choke.

◻—◻—◻

What to remember about "Launch":

- Each morning determines the trajectory for that day.
- Every night, make a list of no more than five things to accomplish the next day.
- Stay away from your phone for as long as possible after you wake up.
- Spend a few minutes making your bed and tidying up in the morning.
- Review the to-do list and add specific people and outcomes to each task.

Actions that require ten minutes or less:

- Make a list of at least one important thing you need to do tomorrow. If you're stumped, go back to your My Legacy email3 and think of ways to collaborate with students, teachers, or both.
- Set a daily calendar reminder for every evening to make your to-do list for the next day. Plug in your phone near the front door, then place the completed list on top of your phone.
- Upon waking, make your bed. Then go back to the list and flesh out any items on it as needed, asking yourself *Why?* and *Who?* for each.

Actions that require thirty minutes or less:

- Write yourself an email with the subject, "My Launch" where you write a single paragraph that describes the perfect morning from the moment you wake up to the moment you accomplish your most important task for the day. Start with the first thing you're going to do when you open your eyes. Finish by describing how you will feel at the end of this perfect morning.

```
┌─────────────────────────────────────────┐
│                                           │
│        CHAPTER  THIRTEEN                  │
│                                           │
└─────────────────────────────────────────┘
                    │
┌─────────────────────────────────────────┐
│                                           │
│              DODGE                        │
│                                           │
└─────────────────────────────────────────┘
```

HOW CAN I AVOID ALL THE DISTRACTIONS OF THE DIGITAL WORLD?

"There are always distractions, if you allow them."

—TONY LA RUSSA, AMERICAN BASEBALL PLAYER AND MANAGER

Simple changes have a big impact on your life. Launching your day is a fantastic first step, but it's just that: a first step. Momentum by itself will not take you all the way to your goals. You cannot build a successful daily routine without another critical ingredient: freedom from distraction.

As we learned in Chapter One, choking is the enemy of purpose. To accomplish our missions, we must be able to dodge the distractions being flung at us. And to dodge effectively, we must take control of the habits and devices that connect us to the digital world.

We've already discussed the first example of this in the last chapter—move your phone away from your bed. That simple change helps you avoid distractions when you're going to sleep and waking up.

Don't take things too far, though. I'm not saying you should get rid of your phone, tablet, or laptop. That's not practical. As tempting as it sounds sometimes, we can't just unplug. All these new connected products are great when we use them purposefully.

Instead of trying to cut ourselves off from the digital world, we can harness it. Focus on carving out specific times during the day when we remove ourselves temporarily from all the background noise. All we need is *some* time to ourselves, the tiniest island of tranquility in a sea of endless content.

AIR TRAVEL

I actually practice using my iPhone in just such a productive way. All it takes is three steps that I can do in about ten seconds. I hold my phone lightly in my hand and slide the little lever on the side so it's on the vibrate setting. Then I swipe up from the bottom of the screen, so I can see the shortcut menu. Then I tap the button to turn on airplane mode. That ensures I won't get any incoming cell signal or a wireless network. In other words, I'm unplugged from the digital world.

With airplane mode on, I press the timer button, which is also on the shortcut menu. I have some timers pre-set: fifteen, thirty, and forty-five minutes. I choose whichever one makes the most sense based on the time of day and task I'm about to do. Then I turn the phone *face down*— that's a good habit to be in—and gently place it on the table. After that, I crank through the most important task from my to-do list. If I need to work on my laptop, I also turn off the Wi-Fi so I don't get distracted there, either.

If I finish early—and I almost always do without distractions—I may move on to another task or turn my phone back on. Sometimes I just sit quietly and enjoy a little peace.

I engage in this weird little ritual from start to finish as often as I can, ideally two or three times a day. It's a tangible reminder that I am in control of my exposure to the digital world.

The inspiration to do this came from stories about how stressed-out people sometimes have a hard time dialing 9-1-1 because they are so shaky from adrenaline and cortisol.* Some vigilant folks—mostly first responders like firemen or police—train their families to dial 9-1-1 so they don't freak out in an emergency. It sounds ridiculous until you end up in a situation like that and realize how much of your reactions in the moment are conditioned by nothing but instinct.

My phone ritual is one of the only consistent ways I've found to dodge the distractions of the digital world. By practicing this pre-determined sequence of actions, I am counteracting the bad habits I've formed with all the screens around me.

How many times a day do you pull out your phone and check your email or social media for no reason? It's a terrible habit! So we need to find ways to neutralize those itchy thumbs.

SCREEN ADDICTS

Phones, watches, laptops, and all the increasing range of connected devices are not going away. Instead, they will grow in availability and sophistication. Beckoning us. Teasing us. Taunting us with a never-ending supply of mindless entertainment.

---

* That is one of many interesting anecdotes in Dave Grossman's book, *On Killing: The Psychological Cost of Learning to Kill in War and Society.*

You and I will turn to that screen almost every time. We can't help it—we're addicted. And like an addict, we trick ourselves with the same tired arguments. What's the harm in a quick peek at Instagram or scrolling through a few emails? After all, it will only be for a second, and then I'll get right back to work.

Except that you won't. None of us do. One of two things will happen. You will get lost in the digital world and never come back to your original task, or you will return to complete the task with a drastic increase in the overall stress, frustration, and effort required.* Neither of those options appeal to me. So I practice disconnecting from the digital world for at least fifteen minutes at a time.

Another compelling reason to dodge distractions in this systematic way is willpower. Specifically, the effect of temptations on our willpower each day. Studies have conclusively shown that we only have so much self-control.[1] Every difficult decision we make saps our energy in a phenomenon referred to as ego depletion.

That's why you may not want to keep cookies at your desk. It's certainly why I don't keep jars of peanut butter around my house! I would constantly be resisting temp-

---

* That is one of many interesting anecdotes in Dave Grossman's book, *On Killing: The Psychological Cost of Learning to Kill in War and Society*.

tation, which would leave me with less energy to tackle the next issue.

That's why we shouldn't keep our phone near our bed or face up on your desk where you can see it.

Resisting temptations drains us each time we are forced to do it. Our goal is clear. We should try to avoid the temptation entirely. That lets us keep our willpower in reserve for those unavoidable moments when we need it the most.

LIFE'S FRICTION

Compare our battle with distraction to basic concepts in physics. An object—or a person—in motion stays in motion unless acted upon by an outside force. We are generating momentum by launching, which takes a lot of energy. That should let us speed through the day, right? Wrong. We are also acted upon by an outside force: distractions.

Distractions act like friction, slowing down the object—in this case, your momentum toward your goals. If there is too much friction, soon there won't be any momentum at all.* A productive life must make every attempt to minimize the friction, so we can get as far away as possible from distractions.

---

* I understand it's not really physics. But it happens to be a great metaphor.

A distracted life merely embraces the friction. Mostly because there never was a destination worth going to, or people who cared when you arrived.

Reducing friction means dodging distractions. You should be acting like Neo during that epic rooftop scene in *The Matrix*.* You're avoiding every possible distraction being "fired" at you. All the notifications, the calendar invites, the calls, the emails, and the messages. Every buzzing, flashing distraction is another bullet headed toward you. And you're avoiding as many of them as possible.

Once the first distraction hits you, you start to lose speed. As your momentum slows, more distractions find their mark. The cycle repeats itself, and before you know it, you've stalled. It's over. You're not going to accomplish anything fulfilling or creative for the rest of the day.

Try again tomorrow.

All of us experience this feeling. What happens when you wake up and immediately check your phone? Suddenly, you are swamped with other people's priorities. Their issues, concerns, problems, goals, needs, and desires. It's all about them and what they want, while your goals get shoved to the bottom of the pile.

---

*   Great scene, one of my favorites: https://youtu.be/xZoOUq_kDh8

Bottom line: distractions are bad. Hopefully, you get it by now. So how to dodge them? We already talked about one specific example—putting your phone on airplane mode for a short period of time—but I want to explain the principles behind it, and why it works. Then you can get creative with your own day!

Let's explore three simple but powerful techniques: minimize screen time, minimize distractions, and recharge yourself throughout the day.

MINIMIZE SCREEN TIME

It's hard to stay away once you check your phone. After that, you feel compelled to go back again and again. Now you are *expecting* replies, likes, comments, and so on. We all identify with that burning desire to dive back into the digital world and bathe in all those fake interactions. Remember, it was designed that way![2]

That's why you need to plug in your phone near the front door, not next to your bed. Avoid plugging into the digital world for as long as possible. Yes, you can always lie to yourself and say this behavior is actually accomplishing something. But deep down, you know it isn't.

In the last chapter, we focused on phones. Now we are talking about much more. We are talking about *all* connected devices, anything that plugs you into the internet. Most of us plug into the digital world even when it's not the most appropriate tool for the job.

As the saying goes, to a guy with a hammer, everything looks like a nail. And so we use our watches, tablets, phones, and laptops all the time without asking whether it even makes sense to start that way.

Let's say you are starting a new work project. Stay away from the computer!

Why? Because the first ideas out of your head usually aren't very good, but those become the foundation for the project if you jump right in based on your initial Google searches. You anchor to your first few sloppy thoughts.

Remember the MVP concept?[3] The first thing you come up with is a guess, not the correct answer. Don't fall in love with the first version of your idea. Instead, try starting with a piece of paper and pencil or a whiteboard. Start sketching out some of your basic ideas. Take your time. The internet isn't going anywhere.

Sketching is a fundamentally different experience than searching online. You *know* these ideas will change. When you have questions about something, you jot them down in the margin or make a note nearby. That becomes something you can investigate online once you have finished this first sketch.

All of a sudden, you are using the digital world to answer a question, rather than mindlessly stumbling through a maze of distractions.

Another scenario is taking notes during a meeting. Everyone does this on a computer, which is a huge mistake for three reasons. First, it's annoying to have to listen to the *tap-tap-tap* of everyone's keyboards. Second, it's easier to type than write, so you tend to write down a lot of the irrelevant stuff. Instead of writing down wisdom, we vomit a bunch of disconnected data into a Word doc. Third, using your computer during a meeting usually means you are also online, so you're not fully engaged in the meeting.

Close your laptop. Put down your phone. Take notes on a piece of paper. Why? Because you won't be distracted. You will be more careful about what you write down, and you now have the option of making sketches or diagrams to reinforce the words. Not everything fits nicely into sentence form.

A hidden benefit is you get to revisit your notes and then type up the stuff that's important in retrospect. This reinforces the key ideas in your mind, helping you sort through all the noise that's coming at you.[4] Your boss and colleagues will all be impressed with the increased quality of your thinking and communication.

MINIMIZE DISTRACTIONS

You cannot get around the need for a computer for most of your life. It is an amazing tool, and it would be counterproductive to avoid them. Fortunately for us, a lot of people share this problem of staying focused in the digital world. There are a host of solutions out there for specific problems. Take a minute and see if you can remember an environment where you consistently started choking in the last few days. Is it in the car before you drive? While sitting on the toilet in the bathroom? Or maybe while you're walking to work?

Once you know the distraction you want to remove, Google can quickly direct you to the appropriate resources in the form of a great blog, online course, podcast, or some other amazing content by a world-class expert on the topic.

That's one of the incredible benefits of the digital world: someone has figured it out and is willing to be your teacher. You just need to stay focused long enough to consume, digest, and apply that information in your life.

Technology changes quickly, and so does the nature of digital distraction. I will not suggest specific programs, tools, or extensions in this book because they will already be outdated. If you are interested in learning more about the best options for your particular needs, go to my collection on the website Product Hunt.[5] I will maintain an updated list there, but you can always find options on your own.

Remember that accessing information is not the problem. Taking meaningful action[6] is the problem. The point is that you can customize your experience in the digital world using tools that others have built for that exact purpose.

RECHARGE YOURSELF

Dodging is all about maintaining the momentum from your launch. You will be bearing down on your daily goals, fired up to have an impact. This type of purposeful life can be exhausting, just like any other activity that demands a lot of your body and mind. You will become more susceptible to distractions as your energy levels decline throughout the day. Fortunately, there are options to help you restock your energy levels.

The most practical way to quickly recharge is a mindfulness practice, which encompasses a variety of activities, including meditation and prayer. Dr. Emma Seppälä[7] is at the forefront of this research and practice. She does a lot of work with veterans who return from war with Post-

Traumatic Stress Disorder and other mental conditions, which is how I became aware of her.

Dr. Seppälä's research builds on a huge body of existing medical evidence that confirms some important benefits about meditation: increased positive emotions, increased life satisfaction, increased memory, boosted social connection, increased resiliency, decreased anxiety, and decreased rates of depression.[8]

For our purposes, focus on the benefit of increased resiliency. That's why you should develop a mindfulness practice. We must be able to repair ourselves quickly. If we can't stay refreshed, we won't maintain the mindset and daily habits that propels us to a purposeful life.

Does mindfulness mean lighting candles and playing soft instrumental music while you sit on a big pillow? No! It can be something as simple as closing your eyes and taking ten deep breaths, counting out five seconds while you inhale and five seconds as you exhale. Or, it could be walking around the block without your phone and quietly observing the world around you. You will be surprised how rested you can feel after a few minutes unplugged.

Like many people, I was a skeptic about this stuff at first. But I decided to give it a shot. I decided to go all out and see if I noticed a serious difference, so I spent ten days at a silent meditation retreat in the backwoods of Northern California.[9] That completely changed my mind. I slept, ate, and felt better during those ten days than any other time in my adult life.

But you don't need a ten-day retreat. The most practical advice about mindfulness comes from marketing guru Seth Godin during an interview with internet celebrity Tim Ferriss. He describes the foundation of any good meditation practice, showing you how easy it can be. "I'll just sit, and I'll close my eyes, and I'll breathe. And when I've had enough of that, I'll go back to what I was doing."*

Simple enough, right?

When you need to be connected, be connected. But remember to carve out time and space for you and all the things you care about. This is especially important at the beginning and end of every day. And don't forget to occasionally take a break to replenish your energy and enthusiasm.

Be aware. Come at each day strong from the beginning and preserve your momentum as much as possible. Launch and dodge!

▣—▣—▣

---

* Seth talks about meditation at 1:50: http://fourhourworkweek.com/2016/02/10/seth-godin/

What to remember about "Dodge":

- Dodging lets us keep up that momentum from a good launch.
- Reduce your screen time by staying away from your computers.
- Reduce the likelihood that you will be distracted during screen time.
- Periodically stop and recharge yourself throughout the day.

Actions that require less than ten minutes:

- Write yourself an email with the subject line, "My Environment" and choose one distraction to remove from your life, when you're going to remove it, and what the penalty will be if you fail to follow through.
- When you are beginning your next work session, organize your workspace and place your to-do list in front of you, so it's easily visible. Place your phone on vibrate or, better yet, in airplane mode. Turn down your computer's volume, too.

Actions that require less than thirty minutes:

- Choose an environment where you are often distracted. Identify a new place where you can move to, or commit to specific ways you can reshape that environment to make it less distracting (keeping your phone on vibrate or wearing headphones, for example).

- Make a list of activities you always do on a computer. Identify a way to accomplish that task without relying on a computer, at least for the initial phases of the activity. Schedule a time to try this new computer-less activity in the next few days.

```
┌─────────────────────────────────────┐
│                                     │
│   C H A P T E R   F O U R T E E N   │
│                                     │
└─────────────────────────────────────┘
                    │
┌─────────────────────────────────────┐
│                                     │
│            TRAIN                    │
│                                     │
└─────────────────────────────────────┘
```

W H A T   W I L L   I T   T A K E
F O R   A   R E S E T   T O
T R A N S F O R M   M Y   L I F E ?

*"Continuous effort, not strength or intelligence, is
the key to unlocking one's potential."*

—SIR WINSTON CHURCHILL, BRITISH POLITICIAN AND AUTHOR

Living with purpose is the best possible gift to give yourself.
Hopefully you know why, and you're starting to see how.
Living with purpose requires the integration of everything
we've learned into a framework you can apply to your life.

Every. Single. Day.

Supercharging works because we inspire ourselves and

others when we play to our strengths. Rallying works because we push ourselves harder and longer when our daily efforts involve other people. Launching works because we need to build momentum toward our goals. Dodging works because we need to avoid the friction that destroys that momentum.

What else do we need? We need to train. Why? Because we live our lives one day at a time. Without a routine, there is no Reset.

The most fundamental changes—the most powerful changes—in our lives are the ones we make in our routines. Daily routines are where the rubber meets the road. And this is where things will start to get hard.

As we change our routines, we feel the pain of sacrificing the comfortable and familiar. It's immediate. Yet the rewards from those same changes are still a long way off. We get frustrated, stumble, then struggle to get back on track. And each time we stumble, there is a chance we just give up.

Our old self beckons to us. Stop trying. Give up. And so we often do. We don't want to change as much as we want to be comfortable. We don't want to train.

To be blunt, if you don't see the value of training, you will probably not make the necessary adjustments to your daily routine. You must embrace training as a way—*the* way—to help you construct a purposeful and fulfilling life.

Remember that success is something we earn slowly. It is built on the accumulated value of our behavior, not the photoshopped lies you see online. Success is not winning the lottery. Success is a grind. And that is why it requires dedication.

CLIMB THE MOUNTAIN

One of my friends, Gunnar—besides having the coolest name in the world—runs a startup called Fidelis Education.[1] For the logo, he chose a profile shot of K2, the most dangerous mountain in the world. For every four people who make it to the top, one person dies trying.[2] Climbing a mountain is Gunnar's metaphor for life and for business. And it perfectly captures the rationale for training.

Climbing is tough work. You can plan all you want but there is no replacement for practical experience. Other people can try to help you deal with it, but at the end of the day, it's going to be you who is cold, tired, and hungry. You will be the one slogging through the switchbacks and false peaks along the way. And you will know that each step brings you a small but meaningful distance closer to the top.

Peaking a mountain can be even more challenging psychologically than it is physically. You don't know you're at the top until you're there. You could be just a few hundred feet from the end and not know it. That's why you need to keep pushing forward even if there isn't a direct line of sight to the end.

DAILY GRIND

Training is similar to climbing a mountain. We need daily discipline because it takes us closer and closer to our goals, even when we can't clearly see the progress. A powerful combination of the push—our willpower and bias toward action—and the pull—our mission and success structure—propels us forward.

It's easy to get overwhelmed when you consider the long and difficult journeys that stand between you and your goals. Whatever dreams are locked inside you, though, can become a reality. Once you embrace the grind, then no set of obstacles can scare you or take away your motivation. And then you're unstoppable.

When you finally reach the peak of a mountain and look down, you can see your trail as a distinct line. That's your journey, laid out behind you in a way that makes it seem simple and clear. But it only looks like that once you're done. The path emerges upon completion. You have to get to the top through daily effort, not by wishing for the perfect set of directions and someone to carry all your stuff.

Steve Jobs, the infamous entrepreneur and creative force behind Apple's incredible success, believed in this approach. "You can't connect the dots looking forward," he said. "You can only connect them looking backward. So you have to trust that the dots will somehow connect in your future."[3]

Just start walking.

TRAIN TO GROW

Training works in many areas. The student entrepreneurs in Stanford's SVIA program learn how to train. Instead of their body and mind, though, it's their business. But the same rules apply. These folks also have to embrace and conquer their own unique grind.

Each entrepreneur starts with a concept for a business and a few other people who believe that this is valuable enough to work on. What they have is actually nothing more than a loose collection of guesses. As described in Chapter Six, we spend the summer showing them how to systematically replace those guesses with facts by getting outside the building and talking to people about their idea. Lots and lots of people, including plenty who disagree with them and slam the door in their face.

Here's how it works. Each team writes out their guesses on the Business Model Canvas,[4] a tool developed specifically to help entrepreneurs capture their guesses about a business and then systematically record their learnings over time.[5] They write out all their assumptions during the first week, then start talking to the people who will pay them. Or more accurately, the teams start talking to the people they *think* will pay them.

Everyone quickly learns that their idea needs a lot of work. The customers are different than they guessed. The problem is different than they guessed. The price is different than they guessed. Everything seems to be falling apart.

At first, this seems bad. Their beautiful idea is being torn to shreds! But they quickly realize how important it is to keep talking to potential customers. Engaging customers is the best way to improve their idea and deepen their understanding of the problem they're trying to solve.

Eventually, the dynamic changes for the entrepreneurs. They start to recognize trends. They believe they can find a good opportunity, even if it doesn't look anything like the original idea.

This simple tactic—customer interviews—practiced over and over is getting them closer to something that is the foundation of a great business. One foot in front of the other, slowly but surely. Day after day after day. They are climbing the mountain!

LITTLE BY LITTLE

Kaizen is a powerful Japanese concept.[6] The word can be loosely translated as "change for better," and it has come to mean a particular kind of continuous improvement that has been adopted by businesses and even people with remarkable results.[7] The core concept is that we can unlock gigantic improvements by focusing on tiny changes over a long period of time. That can mean doing something better or getting rid of something that doesn't work. A little bit at a time. Again and again and again.

Productivity and behavior expert James Clear wrote about the British cycling team and how their coach Dave Brailsford used *kaizen* to take the team from an also-ran to winning their first-ever Tour de France in just three years.[8] Tiny improvements, day after day. That's the power of *kaizen*.

SMALL CHANGES = BIG REWARDS

This concept has many applications for us in our daily behaviors. Imagine a scenario where you spend hours every day glued to your phone, scrolling through social media feeds. You feel trapped by this compulsive behavior, but you know it would make a huge difference if you could control it.

An unhelpful strategy would be trying to cut out social media entirely. We both know that won't work. Instead, focus on making small changes. Take your time progressing toward the ultimate objective rather than being overwhelmed by it. A good place to start would be noticing how much time you spend choking.

Note the length of time. Let's say it's twenty minutes at a time. Could you reduce the amount of time you spend on social media by five minutes each time? Maybe. What about just *one minute* per day? Certainly. So set your timer for nineteen minutes this week, and start the clock each time you go online. Then reduce that time to eighteen minutes per day next week, and seventeen the week after that.

One minute per day. A steady erosion of this bad habit. And yet, magically, five months later, you would be down to zero minutes of compulsive time on social media.

Another *kaizen* approach would be cutting out just one social media feed. You could try uninstalling Instagram for a week. If that felt like too much, you could just change the notifications setting—here's the Android version[9] and the Apple version[10]—so you won't get an alert every time your friends post something.

Simple and not too painful. But it's a start.

TRAINING DAY

Contrast *kaizen* with the way we tend to approach big changes in our life. A New Year's resolution to get in better shape, for example. We want to make progress as soon as possible while our enthusiasm is high. We punish ourselves mercilessly. We cut out all fatty foods, or simple carbohydrates, or both. We spend hours in the gym. We are up at 5:00 a.m. every morning for our jog.

At least that's what we do in early January. By the end of the month, we are back on the couch eating Pringles.

Kaizen training to get in better shape would look very different. Life is a marathon, not a sprint. So we can start small by scheduling a time every day when you want to be more active. Ideally, we would associate the activity with something we consistently do, like brushing our teeth or having lunch.

Set a baseline the first time. Try doing squats without any weight, noting how many you can do. Then try to do one more repetition each successive day, taking a break on the weekends: ten on Monday, eleven on Tuesday, twelve on Wednesday, thirteen on Thursday, fourteen on Friday, then fifteen the following Monday, and so on.

That's it.

Here's another example that involves both physical and social *kaizen*. Schedule a long walk with your spouse or a friend once a week when you know you will both be available. Start with one mile, then do a mile and a quarter. Then a mile and a half. Keep increasing the distance, slowly but surely. Let the conversation distract you from the exercise. Focus on consistency and iterative improvement.

You could also apply the training mindset to nutrition. Do you eat dessert five times a week? Try to cut down four times in January by replacing the dessert with another activity that also satisfies you, such as watching your favorite TV show or face timing with a close friend.

You could reduce dessert intake to three times a week in February. Then drop it again to twice a week in March, and then focus on having a special dessert night once a week after that. No need to cut it out entirely unless that's something you decide to do when you get to that point.

Training every day should not scare you. It should inspire you. When you train correctly, you are doing simple things a little bit better, over and over. That is the reason why Gunnar chose K2 as his company's logo. To climb a mountain, all you need is to take a lot of little steps. Of course, the journey can be difficult, but that's not the same thing as impossible. Not if you keep going.

So train. Today. Tomorrow. The resulting confidence will seep into your soul and never go away.

▣—▣—▣

What to remember about "Train":

- Training is the daily methodology that takes us to our goals.
- Small tweaks will lead to massive improvements over time.
- Stay simple because complex systems are hard to follow.

Actions that require less than thirty minutes:

- Go back to the environments that distract you from "Dodge." Write down an easy first step you could take to reduce the time you spend in each environment. Then identify the incremental steps that will take you toward your ultimate goal of minimizing distractions.
- Go back to your areas of potential mastery from "Supercharge." Write down the fundamental skills you need to develop, and the daily actions that will let you build that skill. Schedule a time to set a baseline

for yourself on each action so you know where you're starting. Commit to a small daily improvement to the baseline.

· Reflect on the last few times you have tried to make big changes in your life. Write down the goal that you had, what you did, and why you think it didn't work. Below that, write down a daily action that is related to these goals. Identify a small improvement to that action, how much time it would take to practice this action each day, and the practical benefits to your daily life.

CHAPTER FIFTEEN

CELEBRATE

WHEN DO I GET TO ADMIRE MY WORK?

"Every day I feel is a blessing from God. And I consider it a new beginning. Yeah, everything is beautiful."

—PRINCE, AMERICAN MUSICIAN AND SONGWRITER

My friend Tariq had an unusual upbringing. His parents were part of a tight-knit black community in Washington, DC. Tariq and his brothers spent their childhood doing community service projects, going out on camping trips, and being educated about their distinct identity and legacy.

Education was the bedrock of Tariq's childhood. One of the culminating events of his early life was high school graduation. His family emigrated from Cuba, and in Cuban culture, Tariq going off to college was a huge deal. Massive, really.

The entire community was invited to a blow-out party to celebrate Tariq's graduation. There was a gift-giving ceremony to commemorate the day. In front of everyone, his dad gave him a sack that was traditionally used by Cuban sugar cane workers. The bag contained a machete and some other tools, each with its own significance. Tariq's dad made the most of the occasion, explaining the full story of every item in the bag.

This ritual was obviously an important symbolic gesture for his dad. He stood proudly in front of the community, talking about his son and the legacy of their family. Tariq waited for him to finish with the impatience of a teenage male who wants to go hang out with his friends.

Tariq didn't understand or appreciate this gesture at the time, but now he is so grateful for the memory of that day. It's an important connection to his past, which gives him deeper confidence in his identity as a man, a member of his family, and as part of a larger community with shared history and values.

Graduations are often a big deal for families, especially if they choose to put a lot of emphasis on education. Even if high school is only an intermediate step before college and then perhaps graduate school, it is still worth celebrating. Financially and socially, Tariq's father went out of his way to commemorate this milestone. And we all have something to learn from this profound act.

END OF TOUR

Despite its conservative brand, the military is surprisingly good at celebrations. Military leaders learned a long time ago about the importance of taking an occasional break to blow off some steam. It takes creativity to keep people at the top of their game. And the stakes don't get any higher than war.

The most common example of a military celebration is when someone leaves a unit. This comes at the end of a tour of duty, which is usually three years in the American military. Everyone in the unit attends, sharing funny or compelling stories about the person. And there is usually some kind of plaque or other symbolic item for the person to keep as a physical token of this period.

These events reinforce the value of the unit's mission and the role each member plays. People tell and retell stories that make up the group's identity. Each story is an exaggerated example of the values they want to pass on to the next generation.

These events allow the older members of the unit to reflect on their legacy and how it needs to be preserved. The younger members of the unit usually sit quietly, like Tariq did at his high school graduation. They may not understand or appreciate the event at the time, but they are still soaking it in.

TIME OFF

Life is about purpose and the people whose lives we touch. And yet the digital world will undermine this perspective by making us feel inadequate. Nothing robs us of our satisfaction like photoshopping. We cannot be proud of our accomplishments while being bombarded by a swarm of humble brags and filtered selfies. Our own accomplishments seem pale in comparison to the imagined lives of our digital "friends."

The reverse is also true, tragically. We share the same types of fantasies in our own social media feeds, with predictable results. Our followers now feel just as inadequate as we do!

Social media erodes everyone's satisfaction, not just yours.

That's the reality of our world right now, yet we still have to find some semblance of balance. Somehow, we must give ourselves regular opportunities to feel good about what we've accomplished by celebrating progress toward our goals. Celebrations restore our souls, renew our commitment, and provide an opportunity to deepen connections with the people we care about.

Except that we don't actually do this. At least the combination of personal experience and data seem to indicate that we don't. Can you believe we take only half of our available vacation time in the United States?[1] Half! That statistic should scare all of us.

We actually seem to avoid celebrations, telling ourselves we'll take a break "later" or "tomorrow," and of course, these days never come. Vacation becomes a shadowy concept, something that exists off in the future. And the fact we will *eventually* take a vacation means we are willing to slave away at work *now*.

By letting us live in an unsustainable way, the concept of vacation has become a toxic influence. We can't outsource fulfillment to two weeks out of the year. And that's especially when we don't take the time off anyway!

A fulfilling life doesn't ask us to behave in an unbalanced way. We can't always be driving forward. Like anything in this world, our progress has a natural rhythm. A flow. There are appropriate times to pause, reflect, and smile. It doesn't matter that there are more challenges waiting for us up ahead. We still need to take stock of where we started and acknowledge how far we've come.

A brief pause can work miracles. The silence lets us appreciate the noise.

GIVING THANKS

After my wife and I wrapped up the first Lagos Garage program in late 2014, we still had a few weeks in Nigeria to spend with her family. Someone at GE suggested we connect with the Tony Elumelu Foundation.[2] This was the charitable arm of a Nigerian billionaire's business empire. The foundation had recently hired an incredibly talented British woman to head their entrepreneurship program. Apparently, she was looking for some experienced people with a background in training and curriculum development.

The initial meeting—which took place the day before we left Nigeria—went well, but we did not have time to follow up in person. The rest of our communication took place via email and Skype. They were trying to figure out if we were good enough to develop the curriculum and content for their flagship effort, a twelve-week training program serving as a *de facto* MBA for 1,000 African entrepreneurs over the next decade.[3]

This was the perfect opportunity for us. We had the

right skillset and on-the-ground experience to build them a program tailored to the reality facing African entrepreneurs. We knew how to deliver on the Tony Elumelu's dramatic vision of developing the continent through entrepreneurship.

After bouncing the proposal back and forth for several weeks, we finally signed a deal in early 2015. It was everything we could have hoped for—a great mission, tight timeline, plenty of resources, and creative space to build something unique. And it was our biggest contract up to that point. My wife and I were on fire!

I remember the moment I turned to tell her the contract was signed, and we were ready to go. We were back in our 380-square-foot apartment in San Francisco. I had this huge smile on my face when I told her. She looked so proud after I gave her the good news. Everything was right with the world. And do you know what we did to commemorate this incredible opportunity and blessing?

Absolutely nothing.

We didn't celebrate at all. No dinner. No day trip. No weekend away together. We just plowed into the program. And we didn't celebrate when we finished, either. We just moved onto the next thing, which turned out to be her job at Apple. That project was the last time we were able to work together.

Looking back, that was one of my biggest mistakes—there are plenty to choose from—in our early marriage. I didn't just miss an important chance to celebrate with my wife. I missed *two*: signing the contract and successfully completing it. I was on track to become one of those worker bees again, so consumed with professional busyness that I never got around to savoring the worthy parts of life.

Why did this happen? Because I was obsessed with applying all the tools of a Reset to prove how much I was capable of. My mission slipped. It became about me, not the hard work of my team or the needs of the thousands of entrepreneurs I was there to serve.

BEGIN AT THE ENDING

These days, I start new projects by planning a party at the end. A good capstone event is critical to the project's overall success, so I make sure to celebrate. Along with the finale, I set up smaller events to correspond with a series of intermediate milestones. Each celebration brings together my team and reminds them all why they are working on this project. It establishes or deepens their connection to one another and to the broader mission. Celebrations are worth it, whatever the cost.

Celebrating is the last piece of the puzzle. Why? Because it confidently predicts that you have something to celebrate. It assumes you will ultimately triumph. That is exactly what you should be expecting once you Reset. Without this belief, you will be stuck trying to prove something. Instead, you should be trusting and enjoying the daily experiences that take you toward a worthwhile objective.

Never underestimate your ability to set and reach goals. You are virtually guaranteed to get there once you have the right mindset, a focus on daily habits, and a support network.

THE TEMPTATIONS

Resetting is hard but worth it. We now understand the level of commitment required for us to find purpose based on a compelling mission, daily action, supportive structure, and a strong community. A lifetime of daily achievement will naturally result if you follow the principles and pathways laid out in this book.

On the other side of your Reset is long-term fulfillment. And that is a wonderful thing. We can all appreciate seeing a pathway toward success. But this is not the whole story. There is danger to Resetting, particularly after we start seeing the fruits of our labor.

Like me during the project for the Tony Elumelu Foundation, you may be tempted to swing the pendulum all the way to the other side. Instead of wasting time in a distracted stupor, we can become obsessed with pushing ahead at all costs. We may start measuring all our activities, treating everything like a work project, and trying to optimize things like quality time with family and close friends. This obsession ultimately diverts us from our true purpose, instead taking us down an unfulfilling path.

There is no contentment in relentless self-improvement or personal accomplishment. We cannot find satisfaction by referring only to ourselves. That is too narrow a view of life, which is why we must constantly involve other people in our daily actions. We can do so much for others. We can teach them, learn from them, or cheer them on. Whatever the activity, our mindset must focus on creating value in the lives of others despite distractions of the digital world.

Ultimately, you are the only person who can choose purpose for yourself. To take on this responsibility, you must create this essential set of missions, actions, structure, and community. That's what it means to Reset.

Remember, success is not about being perfect. Success is about risking some important part of your soul on a worthy cause, day after day. If you're taking meaningful action that benefits others, then you're succeeding. So, be sure to celebrate all along the way. This kind of healthy rhythm will sustain you through life.

□—□—□

What to remember about "Celebrate":

- We have to embrace the natural rhythms of our lives.
- Celebrations are often neglected, but they are incredibly motivating.
- Take time to celebrate in big and small ways for every goal you set.

Actions that require less than thirty minutes:

- Write yourself an email with the subject, "My Success" that lists any of the following goals you want to achieve within the next three months: a physical milestone; a financial milestone; a creative milestone; or a professional milestone. Write down what you will do to celebrate that milestone when it is achieved. Include where and when, and the people you will celebrate with.
- Identify one thing about a friend's life you can celebrate right now. Scroll through social media feeds if you're having trouble coming up with something. Call or message that person. Tell them you want to plan a celebration for them and ask them to name a time

and date when they are free. Invite all your mutual friends if you feel like making it a larger event.

CHAPTER SIXTEEN

EVOLVE

WHEN DOES THE PROCESS END?

"It is not the strongest of the species that survives, nor the most intelligent, but the one most responsive to change."
—CHARLES DARWIN, BRITISH SCIENTIST AND PHILOSOPHER

I always thought I was smart. Or, more specifically, I thought I was quick. I could think and talk on my feet. Unfortunately, I also had a big mouth, which can be an explosive combination, especially for a male teenager.

Without getting into the details, I was kicked out of—excuse me, asked to leave—my first high school about two-thirds of the way through my sophomore year. Not for bad stuff, mind you. The same behavior didn't cause anyone to bat an eye at the large public high school where I restarted school.

Starting over was too much for me, both socially and academically. I didn't see a need for being at school. There was nothing there for me. I could not accept the structure around me—the grading, the attendance, the homework. I rejected it all.

At that point, I gave up on any image of myself as a good student. I let that part of my identity drift away until I forgot I had ever been someone who cared about school. My GPA quickly fell from 3.2 to 1.8. My grades scraped against the bottom fifth percentile of my class for the rest of high school.

Things were bad. My school didn't give me a high school diploma at the graduation ceremony. Instead, I got an empty sleeve with a note reminding me I still had a few credits left to earn before I could graduate. Apparently, there is a limit to the number of classes you can flunk. That sad day was in June of 2000, the culminating black mark of a sad high school experience.

Despite this miserable performance, I ended up receiving my high school diploma after taking some summer classes. This allowed me to qualify for the Marine Corps after I lost enough weight. My military entrance exam scores were high enough to earn a spot in boot camp once I was able to prepare myself physically.

ACCEPTING STRUCTURE

Somehow, I went from completely resisting structure to throwing myself into one of the most structured environments ever built. This was my first clumsy attempt at Resetting. I took responsibility for myself to lose enough weight to get into the Marines. And by doing so, I also learned to appreciate the value of structure in channeling my behavior.

But why did I get started? What was that first mission that drew me toward the Corps? Honestly, my decision probably had something to do with those amazing recruiting commercials with the guy pulling a sword out of the stone.

And then fighting a lava monster.

And then winning.

I am *not* making this up.[1]

Fast-forward four years, and I was getting ready to leave the Marines. Things were going well. At twenty-two years old, I was a non-commissioned officer with responsibility for almost a dozen Marines. I was promoted early on two occasions and had a lot of back-slaps on my way out the door.

But the story sounded different in my head. I was also completely terrified of heading back to school. All I could think about was my last experience as a high school student. I seriously considered staying in the military even though I knew it wasn't what I wanted as a career.

The first visit to a college campus was hardly encouraging. At Cal Poly San Luis Obispo, the admissions folks told me there was no way I could get in. I'm sure there is a rule against laughing at prospective students. That's probably what allowed me to save face as I packed up my transcript and ran out the door.

Remember what we learned in Chapter Five? Don't expect things to be easy as you get started in a new environment.

It soon became obvious that community college was the only option for me. To move ahead with my life, I had to trade a structured environment—the Marine Corps—for a less structured one—school. The rules, norms, and expectations were going to be looser. Now I had some room to adapt to the environment to pursue my goals.

ADAPTING STRUCTURE

Restarting school was not glamorous. I took the assessment test and was promptly placed in remedial classes. Basically, the test showed I wasn't even ready to enter college as a freshman. I had regressed since high school.

I enrolled in two classes—math and English. And I worked harder on those classes than any before or since. I was trying to make up for the awful performance during my final two years in high school. I wrote and rewrote essays, double- and triple-checked mathematical problem sets. I went to every office hours. I created or joined multiple study groups for *both* classes.

I threw myself back into school using the same mindset and behavior from the military. The disciplined work paid off. Two years later, I had a 4.0 GPA and my test scores allowed me to transfer into Stanford. I returned to the Marines as a reservist for a deployment to Iraq, then began classes at Stanford. After dropping out briefly for the deployment to Afghanistan—as we discussed in Chapter Seven—I finally finished my degree a few months before my thirtieth birthday.

I was a changed man. A key piece of my identity was back in place. I felt like I could stand toe to toe with my peers who came from elite preparatory schools. Sure, they were eight to ten years younger than me. But the fact that I could sit in the same classes and *contribute*? Wow, that was amazing.

WIDENING YOUR CIRCLE

My sense of self-worth completely changed during this process. Adapting from the military to academia was difficult. I lacked confidence because I had no adult experiences that clearly demonstrated my competence. I still saw myself as an imposter. I had to do the work to *feel* differently, not just understand at an intellectual level that adaptation was possible.

Once I took this responsibility seriously, it was only a matter of time. I was able to adapt to community college and then to Stanford. I learned that I could grow wherever I was planted. Each time I was shoved into the deep end of the pool, I became a little more confident I could swim. And eventually, I just started jumping in without anyone pushing me.

Isaac Asimov, the famous science fiction author, wrote over 400 books. His breadth of expertise was as awe-inspiring as his productivity. Asimov wrote books on topics ranging from biochemistry to history to human biology. How? He kept evolving. "Each time I wrote a book on some subject outside my immediate field," he recalled in an interview, "it gave me courage and incentive to do another one that was perhaps even farther outside the narrow range of my training."

I know many people with stories like this. Starting from an unremarkable position, men and women from diverse backgrounds and nationalities have experienced a radical shift in their sense of personal responsibility. That shift transformed them. Remember Justin getting passed over by the Princeton recruiter? He never forgot that, and many of his achievements derive from the resulting transformation.

Of course, this doesn't mean people such as Justin have an easy path to success. All of us will experience failure many times along the way. But eventually—painfully—we can learn how to direct our own evolution, not just respond to our immediate environment.

INHERITING PURPOSE

I struggled immediately after school. Fresh off my success at Stanford, I didn't think my work life would be that tough. I was twenty-nine years old, working for a startup that was about to disintegrate—although I didn't know that at the time.

I had traded the structure of school for an early-stage company, but I had failed to notice a more subtle shift taking place. My purpose was now tied to the company, not my interests or values. I did not realize it at first, but my missions each day were externally sourced. They felt... imposed on me. Fake somehow.

Of course, I kept on going at work, powered by my daily launch and a structure that let me preserve momentum each day. But my heart wasn't in it. Purpose cannot be found in the outside world. It necessarily resides inside us.

We don't inherit purpose. It's not like eye color or money from a rich uncle.

It would be some time before I learned this lesson. I think my decision to outsource purpose was actually a throwback from my time in the Marines. Back then, I could expect the organization to provide me with a compelling mission every day. But that didn't work out with the startup. I felt like a hollow shell after just a few months.

It wasn't long after my thirtieth birthday that I had had enough. The company was on its last legs. We weren't even being paid anymore! Then a good friend of mine approached me with the thinnest shred of an offer. Would I consider working for him as he started a small company?

I took stock of where I was. It was about six months after graduating college. I couldn't sustain a serious relationship. I turned down a great job opportunity to work at a startup, which then went bankrupt. I was forced to move into my brother's apartment, because I didn't have a place to live. I was burning through my savings.

Things weren't exactly great. But at least I had one saving grace. I knew I could adapt to almost any situation if given a chance. I had enough confidence to assess the situation and not despair. And this new opportunity was appealing. It was not only about adapting my environment but *creating* purpose in my work with others. So I decided to go for it and found a fantastic organization, now called BMNT.[2]

The intervening years have been remarkable. We have a growing group of people who are similarly obsessed with accomplishing our mission. The rate of learning at a purpose-driven company like BMNT is incredible. We are always taking on more than we should with minimal resources, and we're still managing to over-deliver.

I continue to make mistakes, to learn, and to grow. A lot of my work is now focused on assembling the world's most talented engineers to tackle some of the toughest problems facing our soldiers on the battlefield. We call the effort Hacking for Defense, or H4D for short. A big part of my job is constructing the mission and structure that supports these unique teams of people.

I am constantly pushing people to Reset without them even knowing it.

With H4D, I see how people and problems mix together to address a compelling mission for a short period of time, sometimes only for a few weeks. I see how that purpose infects a team, inspiring them to push themselves harder and faster than they ever imagined. I see how much progress they can make by taking action early and often to get feedback on their ideas. And I see how their daily work can be fulfilling, whether they are in an office or out on the front lines.

BACK TO BASICS

It's easy to get overwhelmed when you think about Resetting. Don't fall into the trap of trying to be perfect. Apply what you've learned, however it makes sense to you. Focus on your strengths. Use family and friends for support. Sort out a good morning routine. Build a supportive environment. Start small and build momentum. Find something to celebrate.

Once we know we can succeed, we can look beyond the here and now. The experience of Resetting will quickly build your confidence. It's not enough to think you can do it. You must *know* you can. And this knowledge can only come from experience.

Confidence is the scar tissue of a great Reset.

Eventually, you will start building a completely unique environment, a daily structure tailored to you that you consciously shape as time goes on. That is the ultimate goal. Take on the digital world each day and win. To find purpose in your daily life despite the distractions. Your mindset and habits can start changing today, although it won't be easy. The journey will challenge you in almost every way, but you will be better off for it. You can overcome any obstacles between you and your goals.

◻—◻—◻

What to remember about "Evolve":

- We start by accepting structure, then we start adapting it.
- We start by inheriting purpose, then we start creating it.
- With the confidence of a successful Reset, we can tackle any challenge.
- The digital world is full of possibilities waiting for us to pursue them.

Actions that require less than thirty minutes:

- Review all the emails you have sent to yourself: My Legacy, My Support, My Launch, My Environment, and My Success. Do you see alignment among the various responses? What's missing? What is the first goal? What is the first step you will take toward that first goal?
- Write yourself an email with the subject, "My Future" that describes a twenty-four-hour period five years from now. Be specific. Talk about where you live, the time when you wake up, how you feel, the work you do, and the people around you. Imagine your future self writing a letter back in time, trying to explain why you need to Reset.

CONCLUSION

ARE YOU READY?

"Life has meaning only in the struggle. Triumph or defeat is in the hands of God. So let us celebrate the struggle!"
—STEVIE WONDER, AMERICAN MUSICIAN AND SONGWRITER

The digital world has emerged slowly but surely over the last few decades, and it now affects every aspect of our lives. It's unfolding in small, discrete changes. We start to communicate differently. Then, we start to work differently. And next, we start to think differently.

Information, once scarce, now threatens to overwhelm us. Our old habits—based on scarcity—are counterproductive in this digital world of abundance. Education has not prepared us. Social media whips us into a frenzy over the littlest things. And financial incentives have been distorted to keep us distracted from dawn to dusk.

We must face these changes. Otherwise, they will lead us toward a life of compulsive distraction that leaves nothing behind. We will keep getting caught in this digital trap if we're not careful.

Fortunately, we are not expected to figure out the digital world on our own. Elite groups of entrepreneurs are thriving in the digital world, pointing us toward the correct behaviors. And these lessons are reinforced by similar principles that are the foundations of military culture.

Focus on a compelling mission. Push yourself to take action as quickly as possible. Structure your day to stay on task. Recruit and learn to rely on others.

Your Reset sequence starts with one small step. Acting boldly is the most useful skill in a world of limitless distractions. Purpose follows action as often as action follows purpose, so we can't fall back on the convenient excuses of perfectionism. Just get started.

With our bias toward action in place, we can focus on supercharging ourselves. We will be guided toward our areas of potential mastery by feedback. Then we can develop those unique strengths that inspire others to collaborate on missions of true value to humanity.

A supportive structure lets us keep up the momentum that we developed with bold steps. That's why we have to rally the people around us. If you need to learn something, find a teacher. If you need encouragement, turn to a cheerleader. If you want to reinforce a lesson, find a student.

Success is ultimately determined by our daily behavior. We can launch ourselves each morning, overflowing with energy to tackle the most important tasks we face. And we can dodge the distractions thrown at us by the digital world by creating space away from our devices, and by engaging with them more carefully.

We must be focused on consistency. Small wins over time will eventually make the difference by cultivating deep expertise. And then we will be succeeding every day, no matter what life throws at us. We will be doing exactly what we want to do and doing it well, not choking on the latest pointless notifications on social media.

BRAVE NEW WORLD

A new life is opening up to us if we choose to rise to the challenge. We will become more confident, focused, inspired, and—most important—useful to others. This is the natural consequence of our evolution as we adapt to the digital world and adapt the digital world to us!

Diligence is the price of our newfound freedom. The ever-present risk is sliding backward toward a life of apathy and convenience. That's why we need to lean on the powerful combination of habits, mindset, and community that we discussed in this book.

Your first Reset will not be your last. Whatever mission you choose, the digital world does not stand still. New opportunities will emerge along with new ways to build mastery, and they will create value in the lives of others. And you will pursue them, reshaping your purpose and environment to suit these new goals.

TO INFINITY AND BEYOND

The benefits of the digital world will open up as you gain control over your impulses and your environment. The ability to make an impact on the lives of others, the deep enjoyment of your day-to-day work, the instant access to useful information, a global community, the massive financial opportunities, and all the rest of it.

You do not need anything else to beat the odds and become one of the success stories.

Here are a few facts you probably didn't know. Each one should be enough to blow your mind, and hopefully push the limits of what you believe is possible in your own life.

The world is safer today (whatever day you are reading this) than ever before *in human history*.[1] In 2015, the global poverty rate dropped below 10 percent *for the first time ever*.[2] Scientists are using people's stem cells to *grow them new organs*.[3] Scientists are also experimenting with nanobots—tiny robots—to *target and kill cancer cells*.[4] Google and Ford are working together to develop *cars that drive themselves*.[5] So are Lyft and General Motors.[6]

All kinds of software is being developed right now by *computers that can improve themselves*.[7] In 2005, there were one-billion people connected to the internet, and since then, that number *has almost quadrupled*.[8] There are high-end virtual reality systems you can already buy, or you can use a smartphone and some cardboard to *make your own virtual reality system*.[9]

Kind of overwhelming, isn't it? These amazing changes are all happening right now. Think about that. We really are living in the middle of a special time in history: the emergence and rapid spread of the digital world. The horizons are expanding all around us. All we need is a workable approach to capitalize on these amazing opportunities.

I want you to develop deep confidence in your ability to Reset and then keep evolving. We both know that won't happen by staying distracted and hoping for the best. You have to defy the digital world that wants you to be a spectator.

You need to Reset. That means excavating the missions that excite you with a compelling *Why?* and *Who?* It's time for you to take action and shape your environment so you consistently have a positive impact on the world.

Revolutionize your mind and your behavior.

What are you waiting for?

ACKNOWLEDGMENTS

I already dedicated this book to my mother, but she also needs to be the first person I acknowledge. It was her dedicated support as an editor that allowed Reset to evolve the way it did. She passed away unexpectedly between the editing and publishing of Reset, so I never got to give her a physical copy of the book she helped make a reality. I will treasure special memories of the time writing this book, when we got to know each other in an entirely new way. Thank you, Mom. I could not have done this without you.

My wife was the first person to believe I had something worthy of a full-length book. We were at a conference together in Las Vegas, and I'll never forget the smile that broke out on her face when I suggested I do this for real. So, thank you, My Queen. Reset became a reality because you said, "YES!"

My father, siblings, cousins, aunts, and uncles all contributed to the writing and editing of Reset. They all deserve many more kudos than I can possibly give in one paragraph. Hopefully, it's enough to say I've never been so grateful to be part of a bookish family.

A much larger circle of people served as my support network, sounding board, and feedback loop. I used a combination of a mailing list and closed Facebook group to engage with about 120 people that I won't try to list by name. Each one helped me in some way, whether it was talking to me about the book's themes, editing a chapter on Google Docs, or just encouraging me to keep going. It all mattered.

And finally, thank you, the reader of this book. I wrote Reset for you, after all. Hopefully, it helped you in some small way. That would make the whole effort worthwhile.

Now, onward.

ABOUT THE
AUTHOR

WILLIAM TRESEDER is a cofounder of BMNT, an innovation consultancy headquartered in Silicon Valley. He
has educated and mentored thousands of entrepreneurs
around the world through partners such as Stanford University, GE, and Singularity University, and has helped
governments and large organizations solve hundreds of
problems. William is a former US Marine who served in
both Iraq and Afghanistan. He lives with his wife and children in the San Francisco Bay Area, and he loves to share
lessons learned with others who are striving to improve
themselves and their families.

.

CPSIA information can be obtained
at www.ICGtesting.com
Printed in the USA
FSHW02n0601200918
52417FS